RECIPES
for
REMINISCENCE

The year in food-related memories, activities and tastes

DANNY WALSH

First published in 2013 by

Speechmark Publishing Ltd, Sunningdale House, 43 Caldecotte Lake Drive,

Milton Keynes MK7 8LF, United Kingdom

Tel: +44 (0)1908 277177   Fax: +44 (0)1908 278297

www.speechmark.net

002-5879 Printed in the United Kingdom by CMP (uk) Ltd

British Library Cataloguing in Publication Data
A catalogue record for this book is available from the British Library.

ISBN: 978 0 86388 962 2

ERRATUM

Recipes for Reminiscence
by Danny Walsh

On page 3, please note that the conversion charts should appear as follows:

C	110	120	140	150	160	170	180	200	220	230	240
F	230	248	284	302	320	338	356	392	428	446	464
	Very cool		cool			moderate			hot		V hot

Gas mark	1	2	3	4	5	6	7	8	9	10
C	275	300	325	350	375	400	425	450	475	500
F	135	149	162	176	190	204	218	232	246	260

Grams to ounces (weight)

Oz	1	2	4	8	10	12	16	20
G	28	56	113	226	284	340	454	566

Ounces to mls (liquid)

Oz	1	2	4	6	8	10	12
Ml	30	57	113	170	227	284	341

Contents

Introduction

This book is about exploring our close relationship with food and its preparation, and should be used as a resource for care workers operating in close relationship with their clients. We are what we eat, or so the saying goes, and you can often tell a lot about a person from their dietary habits! For some people food is merely a source of fuel or energy but for many it is a major aspect of their lives, and for those in residential settings, mealtimes can often be one of the most enjoyable and sociable aspects of the day. Because food plays such an important part in our lives it triggers many memories. Linking the activity and reminiscence ideas with recipes further enhances recollection and allows us to re-experience the tastes of the past. Most of the activities here can be undertaken either on a one-to-one basis or as part of a group activity. Undertaking the activities as a group tends to enhance the pleasure and facilitate more discussion and sharing of memories, as well as acting as a social get-together. You can use the book as a weekly schedule or just dip in and out at will. Perhaps the best approach to using this book is to use it as an excuse to have weekly food-themed parties, the preparation for which will give you many excuses for activities in the week prior to the party. In addition to the occasions cited in this book, make note of your clients' birthdays and other special days in order to use these dates as a focus for celebration. These are important landmarks and milestones for your clients and so should be acknowledged. Such events open up other avenues of activity in preparation for the party, with opportunities to get people involved in not only baking and cooking, for example, but also in all other aspects of party preparation such as shopping, peeling the potatoes, laying the table and polishing the silver, as well as organising games, drinks, music and films. In this way the weekly party could become the focus for a frantic bout of weekly activity, at the end of which everyone will be sorely in need of the party to unwind from organising it! Simple recipes can be followed to make meals, sweets, cakes and biscuits and these can be enjoyed together afterwards. Don't forget the clearing-away and washing-up either, as these are also great opportunities to foster social inclusion and shared activity.

Baking and cooking

These days many people buy convenience foods at the supermarket because they are too busy to cook and bake. However, for many of our clients and their parents, baking used to be a major part of the weekly schedule. It was not just an occasional cake but, rather, the week's bread, cakes and puddings. Baking sessions are a great opportunity for clients to show off their knowledge and skills. Sessions can be organised for mornings with a group to make cakes and biscuits for afternoon tea or supper. You could organise this into a weekly baking session by holding a weekly social afternoon or dance to which others are invited. Planning and deciding recipes are then added to the tasks involved in the preparation. Likewise, cooking has many aspects that can include all. Clients with cognitive impairment are easily included and present you with an opportunity to give companionship and praise. Many magazines are full of simple recipes and it is a good idea to check these around festive periods, as they are often full of good seasonal ideas too, not only for baking but also for crafts and quizzes, as well as being a good source of stories for discussion.

Inclusion and choice

Activity is good for many reasons but it is perhaps best when it focuses upon normal, everyday life. This is especially true for those living in care homes. When so much is done for people within a care setting it is easy for them to gain a sense of redundancy. Food presents many opportunities to involve people in the humdrum of ordinary life so that they can retain a sense of belonging, worth and of having a useful role, rather than being merely passive recipients of care. Much can be made of the business of eating. There are many aspects that provide opportunity for inclusion, as we have hinted, and those with limited physical ability and cognitive impairment can easily be included and thus increase their sense of self-worth by sharing an activity with others. Much of this might at first appear difficult because of the constraints of institutional living, but in reality it is not so difficult to at least have somebody tag along with you to help. A little effort and imagination on the part of the care worker is more than compensated for by the very real psychological benefits to the clients. Allowing choice is important too, especially in relation to food. Care workers can get together with clients to generate a list of the clients' preferences and then work to ensure the clients get these preferences now and again.

A note about measurements

Both Metric and Imperial measurements are used according to the particular origins of the recipes. Below are conversion charts to help you adapt the recipes and instructions to your preferred way of cooking and baking. These will act as a rough guide but if in doubt use one of the many online converters available.

C	110	120	140	150	160	170	180	200	220	230	240
F	32	230	248	284	302	320	338	392	428	446	464

| | Very cool | | cool | | moderate | | hot | | V hot |

Gas mark	1	2	3	4	5	6	7	8	9	10
C		275	300	325	350	375	400	425	450	475	500
F		135	149	162	176	190	204	218	232	246	260

Grams to ounces (weight)

Oz	1	2	4	8	10	12	16	20
G	28	56	113	226	284	340	454	566

Ounces to mls (liquid)

Oz	1	2	4	6	8	10	12
Ml	30	57	113	170	227	284	341

The abbreviations used are tsp = teaspoon and tbsp = tablespoon. It is also worth noting that a UK pint (568 ml) is roughly equivalent to 1.2 US pints – which are only 473 ml. However fluid ounces (fl oz) can be treated as equal.

Reminiscence principles

Much has been written elsewhere on this matter, but it is worth just reminding ourselves of some key principles. Like activity, reminiscence is perhaps best when it focuses on normal, everyday life, as opposed to the antics of the rich and famous. For those living in care, those who are isolated or those with failing memory, reminiscence becomes even more important, and working with people's memories in these situations has a positive therapeutic function. As such, reminiscence should be fun, enjoyable and age appropriate and it should foster belonging, sharing and socialisation. The following paragraphs in this section outline some of the obvious benefits.

Our understanding

Listening to and exploring the lives of clients through reminiscence will give us as carers a better understanding of our clients as individuals. We can gain insight into their personalities, likes, dislikes, values, beliefs and unique histories – in short, what makes them tick! Try building up a scrapbook or life story book with each client and their relatives, to help you reminisce with your clients and to understand them better.

Self-esteem

Our clients are the experts on their own pasts. It is a great boost to anyone's self-esteem to be given attention, to be listened to and to have others show an interest in what they say.

Belonging

Sharing reminiscence can unite people by linking them to others of their generation who hold similar memories. Such sharing of common experiences creates a sense of unity and belonging and can help combat feelings of isolation.

Fun

Fun remains a major reason for reminiscence. It can bring great joy to people to re-engage with and share happy memories. This is a major goal of reminiscence and the activities linked to food in this book.

Social skills

Engaging in reminiscence and activity helps to maintain social skills and encourages interaction via the act of sharing. It can encourage quieter members of the group to join in as they receive positive feedback for their contributions and realise that they, too, are being listened to with great interest.

Triggers

It is useful to have a range of visual aids and props available to help trigger the memory and to make reminiscence sessions more fun. Old objects or large pictures are especially useful. Try hunting for old cookery books, an old mincer, an old egg beater or other kitchen equipment. Try your local museum and library and get in contact with local clubs and societies – these can be a valuable source of trigger material. Remember, triggers can encompass all the senses. Sight and hearing are obvious, but touch is equally important, as are smell and taste, and it is the smells and tastes of the past that are especially important to the theme of this book.

RECIPES *for* REMINISCENCE WEEKS 1–52

Fast Food

Puddings

Fish and Chips

Roast Dinner

Indian Food

Week 1 {January 1–7}

Theme
New Year and good luck food

New Year is traditionally a time for making resolutions and starting anew. Many people start diets in the new year in an attempt to lose the weight they have put on by overindulgence at Christmas time. Historically, one of the earliest known New Year's resolutions was linked to food, as people vowed to return borrowed farming tools!

Across the globe, people have special meals on New Year's Day and visit family and friends to wish them well for the new year. For some the day starts with a hangover from their exuberant celebrations on New Year's Eve, fuelling their resolution to drink less and eat more healthily in future. Many foods eaten on New Year's Day in different cultures are associated with bringing luck for the coming year. In Italy, for example, lentils are said to represent coins and thus are eaten to bring prosperity. In other countries it is cabbage, which is said to represent paper money! Pomegranates in Turkey and around the Mediterranean are associated with fertility and 'plenty' and thus form part of traditional New Year meals. In many Eastern cultures rice is eaten as a bringer of prosperity, while in the southern United States black-eyed peas represent coins and are eaten with 'greens', which represent paper money.

In Japan and Asia, long noodles are eaten as representative of a long life, but the noodles have to be sucked into the mouth without breaking! In other cultures, foods in the shape of a ring, such as doughnuts, represent the seamless transition from one year into another and are thought to bring luck. Here are recipes for two good-luck foods to try.

Pomegranate smoothie

Take 1 cup pomegranate juice, 1 cup vanilla low-fat yoghurt and 2 cups frozen berries and put them through the blender until smooth. There are lots of variations you can try, so get the group to invent their own New Year smoothie.

Simple lentil and vegetable soup

Heat 1 tbsp of olive oil in a pan. Add four chopped carrots, a small chopped onion and 1 tsp cumin and cook for 6 minutes or so until browned and tender. Next, add a can of chopped tomatoes, 700 mL vegetable stock, 1 cup dried (or tinned) red lentils and a pinch of black pepper and bring to the boil. Cover and simmer for 15–20 minutes until lentils are tender and then add a pinch of salt and simmer for a further 5 minutes.

Try experimenting with different vegetable mixtures and different lentils. Look up similar recipes that use black-eyed peas.

Activity

Favourite foods

The simplest way to start this activity is just asking each person what their favourite food and drinks are and what they really don't like! Then, simply browse through a selection of household magazines for pictures of food and make a collage using pictures of each client's

Speechmark

favourites. You might like to start making a scrapbook of useful recipes that you find in these magazines. Take note of each client's favourite foods so you can ensure the they get their favourites every now and again. Another good avenue to explore is: 'What is the strangest thing people have eaten?'

Other food-related themes to ask about include ...

- Have people given or been to any dinner parties?

- What are people's cooking skills?

- Has anybody had any major disasters in the kitchen, such as my father putting a trifle in the oven!

- What did people have for breakfast?

- What did people take if they needed a packed lunch?

- What is the best restaurant they have been to?

Activity

If they were a sandwich

This is an enjoyable discussion game that explores how others see us. It demands a certain degree of lateral thinking, but once the idea has been grasped it quickly becomes a source of great fun. One member of the group is chosen to be 'it'! This person's job is to think of another member of the group and then the rest of the group ask 'it' abstract questions to try to find out whom 'it' is thinking of. Examples of questions to ask 'it' are, 'If they were a sandwich what kind of sandwich would they be?' or 'If they were a fruit what kind of fruit would they be?' After everyone has asked 'it' a question, members of the group try to guess who the person is. Once guessed, 'it' then has to explain why he or she sees the other person as a ham and pickle sandwich, a cabbage, a plum or whatever 'its' answers were. Other food-related categories that you can use for the abstract questions are cake, biscuit, soup, sweet, meal, meat, jam, vegetable, soft drink, alcoholic drink, pudding, and so on. Apart from often being hilarious, this activity provides good feedback as to how other people see us and how we come across to others.

This week's excuse for a party!

A lucky New Year's Day tea party!

If New Year's Eve was a bit 'overindulgent', then a sedate tea party might be the thing for New Year's Day. Start with your lentil soup for good luck. You could add noodles to the soup for extra luck! Then have a selection of everyone's favourite sandwiches and, for more luck and prosperity, finish off with a selection of the many different kinds of doughnut you can find at the supermarket. It is a good idea to quarter these so that people can sample a wide variety. Wash it all down of course with some lucky (and healthy) pomegranate juice.

Week 2 January 8–14

Theme

Puddings

Most of us have a sweet tooth and like to indulge ourselves with our favourite puddings every now and again. Indeed, for some people a meal is not a meal unless it is rounded off by a pudding or 'sweet' of some kind. Ask people to share what their favourite puddings are and why they like them so much. Write the list down for future reference so that you can ensure that everyone gets his or her favourite once in a while. Puddings to recall include sponge puddings, trifles, ice creams, fruit-based puddings, rice puddings, jelly and blancmange, and don't forget the cheese and biscuits. Ask people if they can remember 'instant' blancmange-type puddings, which used to be popular. Ask the group about 'exotic' desserts from other countries they might have tried on holiday, such as baklava from Greece. Also, ask people if they can recall their old recipes and how they made them; this provides you with a good excuse to have a baking session later in the week to re-create some of these old recipes. Don't forget to ask about school puddings too – were they really as stodgy as we sometimes recall?

According to the Ministry of Food 'War Cookery Leaflet No 13', puddings and sweets are 'a delightful addition to a main meal but should only be regarded as such'. This leaflet advises encouraging children to eat their meat and vegetables before allowing them their pudding. This was the rule at many schools too, and no matter how much you hated the first course (with its lumpy mashed potatoes and watery cabbage), if you didn't 'clean the plate' you didn't get your pudding. The leaflet also contains some useful recipes for puddings that could be made without using up too much of the precious rationed sugar and fat. It is full of gems, such as raw grated potato pudding, which was flavoured with coffee, ginger or syrup. Other recipes included prune sponge, marmalade pudding and staples such as bread-and-butter pudding. There was also a recipe for potato pastry, which used 8 oz flour, 1 oz fat, 4 oz cooked and mashed potato, and a big pinch of salt and water. The potato and fat were mixed and the flour, salt and a little water were added until the mixture was 'stiff'. Try using this recipe to make some jam tarts and see how people find the pastry. Here are three more recipes to try.

Basic wartime pudding

Take 8 oz flour, 2 oz sugar, 2 oz fat, 1 tsp baking powder, a pinch of salt and water to mix. Beat the fat and sugar into a cream. Add the flour, salt and baking powder and then mix using a little water. Steam the pudding for up to 2 hours. Fruit or flavouring could be added to this pudding to make it more interesting.

Jam roly-poly

Take 100 g self-raising flour, 50 g suet, a pinch of salt and jam of your choice. Mix the flour, salt and suet and a little water into a dough. Roll the dough out flat, about 1 cm thick. Spread the dough all over with jam, roll it up and wrap it loosely in foil. Steam the pudding for about 2 hours.

Spotted dick

Take 75 g self-raising flour, 70 g suet, 50 g breadcrumbs, 50 g sugar, a pinch of salt, 150 g mixed currents and raisins, ½ tsp mixed spice and 150 mL milk. Mix all the dry ingredients together in a bowl and then add the milk to make a dough. Place the dough in a bowl and allow it to rise, and then cover the bowl well with foil and steam for up to 2 hours.

Activity

General food quiz

What does an angel cake do without?
Egg yolks

Where does Emmental cheese come from?
Switzerland

Which nuts are used to make marzipan?
Almonds

Feta cheese comes from?
Greece

What was created by French monks to look like a child's arms folded in prayer?
The pretzel

What can't coeliacs eat?
Gluten

Chapatti and nan are breads from where?
India, Pakistan and south east Asia

What spread is named after a French earthenware cooking pot?
Marmite

What is a tortilla?
A thin Mexican pancake

What herb waits for no man?
Thyme

What kind of cheese is made backwards?
Edam (m-a-d-e)

What did President Reagan's administration controversially class as a vegetable?
Ketchup

What is the only edible rock?
Salt

What pudding's name means burned cream?
Crème brûlée

What cake is traditionally pink and yellow and covered in marzipan?
Battenberg cake

What three flavours make up a Neapolitan ice cream?
Vanilla, strawberry and chocolate

What dessert is named after a ballerina?
Pavlova

What part of the cinnamon tree does the spice come from?
The bark

What animal's milk is used to make mozzarella cheese?
The water buffalo

When were instant mashed potatoes introduced commercially?
1955

Activity

Food as an opportunity for involvement

Fostering independence and involvement is perhaps one of the most important aspects of caring in residential and nursing home settings. One of the important aspects of life is the ability to make decisions and choices, and diet is an important area to consider in this respect. Think about all the activities that go into food, from the grocery shopping through to the final arrival of the food on the table, and you will begin to appreciate the possibilities for choice and involvement. Taking each client in turn, think of all the ways in which the client could have a greater say or could take a larger part in what happens. Ask them if they would like to help with shopping, food preparation, cooking or laying the table, and don't forget the washing-up! There is a certain normality about running out of things and so having to nip to the local shop. Bread and milk are good examples of staples that often need to be bought from the local shop, and we can include the client in these errands. However, there are many more excuses that we can use to include each client in his or her own life via shopping. Clients can shop for personal items such as favourite biscuits and snacks. There is also no reason why residents as a group should not to some degree be involved in a weekly shop in a supermarket, if they so desire.

This week's excuse for a party!

Pudding party

Basically, this is just an excuse to indulge our sweet tooth and try out different recipes. Augment this by taking a few people around the supermarket to look for a range of cheap and easy puddings to add to the evening so that people have a wide range to try on the night. Also look for custard in cartons and tinned milk to have as accompaniments to your home-made puddings.

Week 3

January 15–21

Theme

The 1940s, the war years and making ends meet!

The war years were years of immense upheaval and sadness, and yet out of this adversity came a feeling of togetherness and a fortitude to not give up, to soldier on and to see it through. Part of this philosophy related to food: people dug up their flower beds to grow potatoes, they cultivated waste ground and turned dereliction into allotment. The 1940s housewife was very creative! Rationing came into force in 1940 with limits on sugar, meat, tea, fat, eggs, milk, jam and cheese, to name just a few, and so many inventive recipes came to light. There was even a Minister of Food, Frederick Marquis, 1st earl of Woolton, who gave his name to the 'Woolton pie', which consisted of carrots, parsnips, potatoes, turnips and oatmeal, topped with a pastry or potato crust and served with gravy. More food had to be home-grown, as supply ships were being sunk and there was a shortage of labour on the farms. Women were encouraged to work in the fields and the Women's Land Army was re-formed after being disbanded following the end of the First World War.

Domestic cultivation was encouraged with the famous poster 'Dig for Victory'. There were even farming holiday camps where you could 'lend a hand on the land'. Dried eggs, dried milk and Spam were imported from the United States. For many people, diet improved with rationing, as it meant less sugar and fat and more vegetables. Children were given daily doses of milk, orange juice and cod liver oil to boost their vitamin intake. Rates of tooth decay dropped too, and with petrol rationing people became slimmer, as they were walking more. Here are three 'austerity' meals to try.

Bread and dripping

Bread and dripping was popular because you couldn't afford to waste any food so the little bit of meat you got was put to good use. Later, in periods of industrial unrest in the 1950s, many strikers' families survived for a time on bread and dripping. Frying a few rashers of bacon will yield a surprising amount of dripping, which forms a tasty spread for your bread in the absence of butter. You used to be able to buy dripping at the local butcher, and chip shops used to fry their chips in beef fat, but it is now considered unhealthy. So try out a meal of bread and dripping ... a bacon sandwich without the bacon!

Woolton pie

Put 1 lb diced potatoes, 1 lb chopped cauliflower, 1 lb diced carrots, 1 lb diced swede or parsnip, four chopped spring onions, 1 tsp vegetable extract and 1 tbsp oatmeal into a large pan. Add just enough water to cover the vegetable mixture and then cook for 15 minutes. Allow the vegetable mixture to cool and then put it into a pie dish and sprinkle some chopped parsley over it. Make a pastry out of wholemeal flour, lard and water. Roll the pastry out and use it to cover the pie dish. Bake the pie for 25 minutes and serve it with gravy.

Chicken carcass soup

Place the bones, skin and scraps from a chicken carcass into a pan and cover it with water. Bring it to the boil and then allow it to simmer for up to 3 hours. Leave the soup to cool overnight and it will 'set'. The next day, reheat the soup and bring it to the boil. Strain the bones and skin. Brown a chopped onion in a pan, add it to the soup and boil. Add salt and pepper to taste. This soup is a bit 'fatty' for our modern palate but it would have been a good source of calories in hard times … if you were lucky enough to have a chicken in the first place!

Leftovers …

One common way of making food go further was by using leftovers. 'Bubble and squeak' was perhaps the best-known use of leftovers and it became a firm favourite for many. Ask the group about other ingenious ways of using leftovers and stale bread.

Activity

Lean times and a siege cupboard!

Perhaps only some clients may remember rationing, but all can reflect back upon lean times such as being a student or living away from home with poor wages, when they had to live on a tight budget. What were each client's staples in such times? Can you live on tinned beans alone? Ask your clients if they had to stock up a cupboard for a siege today, what would they put in it? Write up the list on a flip chart. Once you have generated the list, ask what they would keep if they could only have 10 choices.

JANUARY

This week's excuse for a party!

Pack up your troubles ... an austerity party

The idea here is to use rationing party foods and to try to re-create a sort of street party atmosphere. So the background music will be old music hall songs and wartime favourites. Party foods to make are Spam, jam, Marmite and fish-paste sandwiches, along with the following recipes. Glasses of stout or a few tipples of port and lemon will help to get the party going; otherwise, wash it all down with a nice cup of tea!

Wartime trifle

Cut some 'stale' currant buns in half and pour some fruit juice and then some freshly made custard over the buns. Top with any fresh fruit you can get your hands on!

Coconut oatmeal biscuits

Also known as Anzac (Australian and New Zealand Army Corps) biscuits, coconut oatmeal biscuits kept well and were sent to the front in the First World War by wives and sweethearts. Mix 1 cup oats, 1 cup sugar, 1 cup flour and 1 cup shredded coconut in a bowl. Add 8 tbsp butter, 2 tbsp golden syrup and 2 tbsp water to a pan on a low heat and whisk and melt. Stir 1 tsp baking soda into the wet mixture and then pour this onto the dry mixture and combine. Dollop spoonfuls of the combined mixture onto a baking tray and bake the biscuits at around 400°F for 15 minutes.

Week 4 — January 22–28

Theme
Burns Night and Australia

On 25 January 1759 the Scottish poet Robert Burns was born, and this is celebrated by Scots the world over with a Burns Night supper. In addition, 26 January is Australia's national day, which celebrates the landing of the first shipment of convicts at Sydney Cove in 1788. This presents us with an ideal opportunity to look at Antipodean food tastes.

Activity

Burns Night

The Burns Night celebration traditionally has recitals of Burns' poetry and many whisky toasts, as described shortly. Here are a couple of traditional Scottish recipes to make in preparation for the supper.

Cock-a-leekie soup

This traditional soup dates back to the sixteenth century. Place a 'boiling' chicken, with legs and wings attached, in a large pan and cover with water and bring to the boil. Remove any 'scum' that appears and add 1lb leeks, cut into discs 1 cm thick. Add salt and pepper to season and simmer for up to 3 hours. Remove the chicken, strip the meat from the bones, cut the meat into small pieces and return the meat to the soup. Add 1 oz long-grain rice (or pearl barley), ½ cup dried stoned prunes, ½ cup diced carrots, ½ cup chopped celery and a small, diced onion. Simmer for 30 minutes and serve sprinkled with chopped parsley and a few bannocks.

Bannocks (Scottish oatcakes/flatbread)

Mix 4 oz oatmeal (or wholemeal flour), a pinch of salt and ½ tsp bicarbonate of soda in a bowl. Add 2 tsp melted bacon fat and ½ tbsp water and mix into a paste. Divide the paste into two balls and roll each in oatmeal to coat the surface. Flatten the balls to ¼ inch thick and cut each into quarters. You can cook these in a heated, greased frying pan for about 3 minutes on each side or bake at 375°F for 30 minutes on a greased tray.

Activity

Australian food

This activity presents an opportunity both to ask if anyone has ever been to Australia and sampled the fare and to have a general discussion about Australia and whether anyone would like to emigrate there. Themes to act as prompts are Sydney Harbour Bridge, Great Barrier Reef, Ayers Rock, koala bears, kangaroos, the 'outback', 'Waltzing Matilda', Aborigines, Rolf Harris, and so on. Visit a travel agent for brochures and pictures to use for an Australia quiz. Most sources tell us that Australia does not have a national dish, but it does have some favourites. Barbecues, or 'barbies', of steaks and sausage are popular and barbecuing in city backyards is said to give people a feeling of being in the countryside. Kangaroo steaks and shrimps are popular. Those living near the coast enjoy barbies on the beach … even on Christmas Day, as this is in the Australian summer. Australians are also fond of meat pies and Vegemite on toast.

Vegemite is similar to Marmite and is a by-product of the brewing process. This leads us to Australia's other culinary passion … beer! A barbie wouldn't be a barbie without a 'healthy' supply of lager, which should be taken well chilled.

Indoor barbie!

This week is an excuse for an 'Aussie' night with an indoor barbie! Have some sausages, steaks, burgers, chops and shrimps, and serve these with a range of different relishes. Play some Australian music and perhaps watch an Australian film such as *A Town Like Alice* or *Walkabout.* As part of the evening get people to try soldiers of Vegemite on toast and of course … don't forget the beer!

Activity

What price is it?

This is usually an eye-opener and good fun. Borrow a shopping basket from your local supermarket and fill it with tins, boxes and packages from the pantry. The items are then passed around the group for them to try to guess what they are worth. The current price is then revealed. If you can't use the real thing, collect empty boxes, tins and jars to be passed around and ask the clients to give a price for each item while they are holding it. Keep a tally on a flip chart so that you can record who is the nearest. This usually generates much discussion and shock as to how high prices have risen. It is also the springboard for a discussion as to whether the items are worth that much or not. For reminiscence purposes it would be good to have some old pictures or old boxes of these modern versions.

This week's excuse for a party!

Burns Night supper

For this celebration guests are usually piped in, but bagpipe music playing in the background will suffice. The host welcomes the guests and declares the supper open. A special Burns poem, 'The Selkirk Grace', is read aloud.

> Some hae meat and canna eat,
> And some wad eat that want it;
> But we hae meat, and we can eat,
> Sae let the Lord be thankit.

The meal begins with cock-a-leekie soup and flatbread or oatcakes. Then the haggis is piped in from the kitchen while the guests stand and applaud this.

The host reads the Burns poem 'Ode to a Haggis' and then cuts up the haggis. The haggis is served with 'neeps' (swede or turnips) and 'tatties' (potatoes) both boiled and mashed with butter. Scottish oatcakes and cheese are often served as the dessert.

Between each course there are toasts with whisky. The lassies are toasted, the lads are toasted and the Queen is toasted. At the end of the meal Burns poems such as 'My Luve Is Like a Red, Red Rose' or 'The Birks of Aberfeldy' are recited.

This can be followed with some highland dancing and the evening closes with a rousing version of 'Auld Lang Syne' and yet more toasting.

Week 5   January 29 – February 4

Theme

The Chinese New Year and lucky Chinese food

The Chinese New Year is the most important Chinese holiday and is really a 'spring' festival marking the end of winter. It can occur anywhere between late January and early February based upon the phases of the moon in the solar year, and it lasts about 15 days. The Chinese New Year is celebrated in many Eastern countries such as Hong Kong, the Philippines, Malaysia and Taiwan, and of course in many 'Chinatowns' throughout the UK and the rest of the world. There are many regional customs and variations but generally there is much giving of presents, family visiting and decorating of houses and streets, and it is traditional to have a thorough clean of the home to brush away bad luck and to welcome better fortunes. There are dragon dances and processions with ornately made dragons and fireworks. Doors are decorated with red paper cuts and *duilian* or Chinese poetry wishing good fortune to all. The eve of New Year is celebrated with a special feast, with fire crackers let off at the end of the feast. The main message of the Chinese New Year is one of forgiveness, reconciliation and wiping the slate clean.

Some Chinese foods are traditionally seen as lucky, such as Chinese dumplings – these can look like ingots of silver and it is thought that the more you eat the more money you will make in the coming year. Spring rolls are said to represent gold bars while noodles represent a long life. Serving a fish with its head and tail still on is said to represent good fortune lasting all year, that is, from end to end. Serving food wrapped in lettuce is also said to bring luck.

Chinese spring rolls

Heat 4 tbsp vegetable oil in a wok. Add a couple of finely chopped chicken breasts and fry until cooked. Add four finely chopped spring onions, three grated carrots and a grated courgette. Cover the pan, lower the heat and cook for about 5 minutes. Next, add 150 g bean sprouts, 200 g finely chopped water chestnuts and 200 g finely chopped bamboo shoots and cook for another 5 minutes. Stir in 2 tbsp soy sauce, a pinch of salt and a sprinkling of black pepper and then stop cooking.

Cut some sheets of filo pastry into strips about 6 inches by 8 inches. You will need one strip for each roll and this mixture will give you about 16 rolls. On each strip of pastry lay a large tablespoon of filling along the middle. Roll up each strip, fold the ends of the pastry over to seal the roll, and brush the ends with vegetable oil. Bake the rolls for around 15 minutes at 190°C until golden and crisp.

Activity

Seed pictures

All you need for this activity is some PVA glue, stiff coloured card and a selection of lentils, beans, seeds and pasta shapes. Invite your clients to make patterns by using the different shapes, sizes and colours of the seeds, beans. Suggest that they experiment first, to see what the possibilities are, before gluing the seeds, beans, and so forth to the card. No great artistic skill is necessary, as pleasing patterns can be easily created. It is easier to draw a simple pattern onto the paper first and then fill it in with the seeds, beans, and so forth. However, the more adventurous clients might choose to draw a picture and use the seeds, beans, and so forth as mosaic pieces. You can also photocopy a selection of line drawing outlines for clients to fill in like a mosaic. Try decorating plant pots or vases – these can look very effective with natural designs using seeds, beans, and so forth. These can then be varnished.

Activity

'Smartie' auction!

Prior to this game take a trip around your local 'pound shop' and buy as many things as there are clients. Try to get things you think the clients might like or use, such as toiletries or fun items. At the beginning of the session, display all the items for all members of the group to see. Each member has a tube of Smarties and you begin to auction the items you bought. Clients bid for the items using the sweets, with you acting as the auctioneer … going once … going twice … then bang your gavel. Gone!

This week's excuse for a party!

Chinese takeaway night!

Take a trip to your local Chinese take away and buy a selection of dishes so that your group can try a wide variety. If you are on good terms with your local takeaway, try inviting them in to cook a Chinese supper for the clients. Decorate the room by lighting some traditional Chinese lanterns. These are made of rice paper and have a light inside and can be hung around the room. Add to the fun of the evening by supplying everyone with a set of chopsticks – everyone will enjoy the chaos, but some people may be surprised by their dexterity. Take a look around the local Chinese store and see what different drinks there are available to try out too. And don't forget the fortune cookies. These are a crispy biscuit with a piece of paper inside with written words of wisdom or a prediction. Again, these can be sourced from your local Chinese shop or bought online.

JAN – FEB

Week 6

February 5–11

Theme

Tea for two: the post-war years and 1950s

The post-war years were an era of great relief and an attempt to return to normality. However, this was not so easy with rationing not ending until 1954. In this era, people generally ate a less healthy diet as more meat, sugar and fats became available, and the practice of growing your own food declined sharply throughout the 1950s. Increasing numbers of fast-food cafes developed in the late 1950s, and more people owned cars and televisions. By the mid-1950s wages had increased and the economy was growing so much so that, in 1957, the prime minister, Harold Macmillan, told the nation that Britons had 'never had it so good'. The fifties are also remembered as a time when holiday camps such as Butlins were very popular. There was also a burgeoning youth culture and the beginnings of 'rock and roll' and 'Teddy boys', with much hanging around in coffee bars. Elvis Presley became very popular and, with those slightly older, *The Goon Show* became a cult radio comedy show.

Food-wise, electric gadgets such as mixers, blenders and pressure cookers were becoming more available and made life easier in the kitchen. More and more people had refrigerators and so could keep perishable foods longer. With the end of rationing, tea parties became popular, as were corner tea shops and coffee bars. Therefore, this week's recipes are two for tea.

FEBRUARY

Cheese muffins

Beat an egg and stir in ¼ pint of milk, add a pinch of paprika and stir. Sift 90 g flour, 4 tsp baking powder and a pinch of salt together and add 30 g grated cheese. Pour the liquid mixture onto this, beating it hard. Grease some muffin tins and half fill each one and bake at around 400° F.

Chocolate cake

This recipe comes from the 36th edition of *Foulshams Universal Cookery Book* which was first published around 1930 and for many British housewives was a standard reference in the kitchen in the 1950s and beyond. The ingredients are ¼ lb chocolate powder, ½ lb flour, 6 oz margarine, 6 oz castor sugar, 4 tbsp milk, 2 eggs and a ½ tsp bicarbonate of soda. The instructions simply state, 'Mix all the ingredients thoroughly, adding the beaten eggs and milk last. Bake in a hot oven.' You then coat with chocolate icing. The icing is 1 tbsp melted butter mixed with 1 cup icing sugar to which you add 2 oz grated chocolate and sufficient boiling water to make a smooth paste.

Discussion activity

Some notable events of the 1950s

1950	Petrol costs 3 shillings (£0.15p) a litre (in the UK today this is around £1.40 p); Roger Bannister runs a 4-minute mile; *The Archers* and *Andy Pandy* are broadcast for the first time.
1951	The Festival of Britain and the first Miss World competition are held; zebra crossings are launched; *Come Dancing* is shown for the first time.

1952 King George VI dies; the first UK Singles Chart is published; Agatha Christie's The Mousetrap opens in London; Humphrey Bogart and Katharine Hepburn star in The African Queen.

1953 Sweet rationing ends; Queen Elizabeth II crowned; Edmund Hillary and Tensing Norgay conquer Mt Everest; 300 die in flooding on the east coast of England; Stanley Matthews wins his first FA Cup.

1954 The first 'fast food' Wimpy bar opens in London; rationing ends; Lester Piggott wins the Epsom Derby at the age of 18; Jim Reeves dies in an air crash; From Here to Eternity sweeps the board at the Oscars.

1955 The Dam Busters is released; the Guinness Book of Records is first published; Airfix produce their first model kit, a Spitfire.

1956 Grace Kelly marries Prince Rainier III of Monaco; premium bonds go on sale; Marilyn Monroe marries Arthur Miller; the Suez Crisis occurs; Corgi model cars are introduced; Tesco open their first self-service stores.

1957 TV detector vans are introduced; the European Economic Community is formed; the Queen makes her first televised Christmas broadcast; Donald Campbell breaks the world water speed record on Lake Coniston, Cumbria in his Bluebird K7 jet boat. This was his fourth record and he was to go on to break it three more times; Tom Finney is named Footballer of the Year.

1958 Seven 'Busby Babes' die in the Munich air crash; yellow no-parking lines are introduced; 'Great Balls of Fire' is No 1 for Jerry Lee Lewis, as is 'Jailhouse Rock' for Elvis Presley; the Campaign for Nuclear Disarmament is founded.

1959   The first part of the M1 is opened; the Mini car is launched; 'Living Doll' by Cliff Richard is No 1; the first post codes are introduced in the UK; the first motorway service station at Watford Gap opens; the musical panel television show *Juke Box Jury*, chaired by David Jacobs, is launched in the UK.

Activity

Food word search

Find the following words hidden in the grid.

cake, carrot, tea, banana, radish, coffee, crisp, potato, bun, sweet, tart, meat, trifle, jam, toast, trout, milk, sugar, beer, plum.

C	A	K	E	D	R	O	M	E	R
R	A	P	D	I	S	W	E	E	T
I	T	R	O	U	T	F	A	T	O
S	T	A	R	T	F	I	T	L	A
P	R	D	A	O	A	S	T	B	S
P	I	I	C	B	T	T	A	U	T
L	F	S	S	A	E	N	O	N	W
U	L	H	E	J	A	M	I	L	K
M	E	I	F	N	D	B	E	E	R
S	U	G	A	R	G	O	H	A	T

This week's excuse for a party!

Tea party

PARTY TIME

Nothing could be simpler for this tea party: some fifties music, tea in china cups and saucers, your chocolate cake and cheese muffins and a selection of fancy cakes and a few savouries to choose from. Then maybe some dancing, followed by a classic fifties film such as *The African Queen*.

Week 7 February 12–18

Theme

St Valentine's Day and the food of love!

The date 14 February is St Valentine's Day, so the theme for this week must be romance and the food of love. With a history dating back to pagan festivals paying homage to the god of fertility, St Valentine's Day has become an established tradition whereby expressions of devotion are exchanged.

History

The ancient Romans had a festival called Lupercalia on 15 February to celebrate the she-wolf who suckled Romulus and Remus. This involved semi-naked men running around whipping girls with goatskin strips in the belief that this would encourage fertility. It developed into a time to meet and court your heart's desire! There are several historical versions of St Valentine and one was a Roman priest who used to marry young couples in secret when Claudius II banned marriage because he couldn't get enough soldiers for his army. Claudius eventually had St Valentine executed on 14 February AD 269 AD. In AD 496 St Valentine was made the patron saint of lovers and thus we have St Valentine's Day. However, there are many variations on St Valentine's story. The Victorians are credited with popularising the Valentine card but the giving of flowers on the day dates back to the sixteenth century, when the ladies of the court were given flowers by their admirers at parties on St Valentine's Day. The association with chocolate dates back even further, as the Aztec emperor Montezuma used to drink chocolate daily in order to fulfil his 'obligations' to his many wives!

The food of love!

The Greek goddess of love, Aphrodite, gives her name to the word aphrodisiac for substances that are said to make us feel more amorous! Here are some examples.

- Alcohol. Alcohol decreases inhibition and increases desire but limits performance!
- Almonds. The aroma of almonds is thought to induce passion.
- Aniseed. The ancient Greeks used aniseed as an aphrodisiac.
- Asparagus. Bridegrooms used to be fed asparagus as an aphrodisiac in nineteenth-century France.
- Avocado. The Aztecs used to call the avocado tree the 'testicle tree'!
- Caviar. Caviar is a well-known aphrodisiac, if you can afford it.
- Chocolate. Chocolate certainly gives you more energy, and apparently Casanova preferred it to champagne (no taste, some people).
- Garlic. Garlic increases desire, but the smell would put you off!
- Honey. Mead used to be given to honeymooners.
- Oysters. Oysters have been used as an aphrodisiac since ancient Roman times.
- Strawberries. Strawberries are considered the ideal food to hand-feed your lover!
- Vanilla. The scent of vanilla is said to increase desire.

Chocolate truffles

What could be better than to make your own traditional valentine gift? Place 120 g unsalted butter and 175 g icing sugar in a bowl and stir until well mixed. Add 2 tbsp cocoa powder and 1 tbsp rum and mix. Shape spoonfuls of the mixture into balls and roll them in chocolate shavings. Roll some in white chocolate shavings too and some in chocolate hundreds and thousands. Add an almond to the top of each truffle. Refrigerate the truffles for an hour and … enjoy … or give to your 'someone special'!

Activity

My funny valentine!

There are many possible avenues to explore here, such as cards people have sent, the joy of receiving a valentine card and the embarrassment of not receiving one. Can people recall St Valentine's Day dances they went to? Here are some other areas to explore.

- Childhood sweethearts.
- Who was your first girlfriend or boyfriend?
- What restrictions were clients under with regard to seeing boys or girls and going out?
- What advice, if any, did your mother or father give you about the birds and the bees?
- Can you remember your first date and your first kiss?
- How did you meet your spouse or partner?
- Two pertinent questions to ask: 'What is the most romantic thing you have ever done?' and 'What is the most romantic thing that has ever happened to you?'

To act as triggers it would be worth getting a few modern valentine cards to pass around and read out, as they often have witty and somewhat 'racy' verses.

Activity

Anagrams of food

This activity is easy to organise and can be varied in degree of difficulty, from the (uvisobo) obvious to the (lossebiimp) impossible. The leader writes the anagrams on a flip chart and the group have to work them out. You could do it together or divide the group into teams. Here are a few examples.

Chinsap	Spinach
Cier	Rice
Lifter	Trifle
Trocar	Carrot
Ucitibs	Biscuit
Noircaam	Macaroni
Dewse	Swede
Dreab	Bread
Abbecag	Cabbage
Uprint	Turnip
Ppoolill	Lollipop
Seeech	Cheese

FEBRUARY

This week's excuse for a party!

Valentines party

'Tis better to have loved and lost than never to have loved at all.

Alfred, Lord Tennyson

A valentine's tea and dance will give you an excuse for some group work. Ask the group to decide on how to decorate the room, what flowers to display, what music to play and what food to have. Make it a simple sandwiches, snacks and cakes affair, as this will give you the opportunity to do some baking with people and make a trip to the supermarket for other cakes and savouries. After the tea and dancing it might be nice to sit down together and round off the evening by watching an old romantic 'weepie'! How about *Brief Encounter* or *Casablanca*, or for something more modern try *Before Sunrise* and *Before Sunset*.

Week 8　　　　　　February 19–25

Theme

New gadgets, 'new' food and the Swinging Sixties!

The sixties were a time of great change and a growing youth culture with the 'hippie' movement. 'Carnaby Street' fashions such as the miniskirt, as modelled by Twiggy, spread very quickly. The Beatles, the Rolling Stones and The Who were among many groups that put Britain at the forefront of the pop music world. The more liberal ideas evolved by this generation have stood the test of time and underpin much of our modern attitude to life. Food-wise, many people had 'new' gadgets such as electric can openers, electric mixers, liquidisers and non-stick frying pans. The popularity of refrigerators meant that people didn't have to go shopping so often, and in the late 1960s freezers were also becoming popular. Before long, frozen peas were the best-selling vegetable. Fizzy drinks began appearing in cans instead of bottles, coffee was becoming as popular as tea and the number and variety of 'takeaways' was increasing – in particular, Chinese. With the popularity of TV cookery programmes such as Fanny Cradock's series, people were also becoming more adventurous in their tastes and cooking. Dishes such as chicken supreme became popular, as did quiches.

Chicken supreme

Slice two small onions and chop four cloves of garlic and fry these together in olive oil. Separately, fry four chopped chicken breasts until cooked and then add the onion and garlic to this, along with six rashers of fried chopped bacon. To this add one chicken stock cube in

100 mL boiling water. Then add 400 mL of double cream, stir well and heat it up. Serve the meal with rice.

Quiche Lorraine

Line a flan dish with 8 oz shortcrust pastry. Bake the pastry blind for 20 minutes at 400°F. Beat four eggs and add 7 fl oz milk, three slices of chopped cooked bacon, 6 oz grated cheese and season with black pepper. Cover the base with tomato slices and then pour the mix into the flan case. Sprinkle grated cheese over the top and cook at 325°F for about 40 minutes.

Discussion activity

Some notable events of the 1960s

1960   'My Old Man's a Dustman' by Lonnie Donegan is top of the pops; Elvis Presley marries; traffic wardens are introduced; 200,000 copies of *Lady Chatterley's Lover* are sold on the day of publication; the first episode of *Coronation Street* is screened.

1961   The contraceptive pill becomes available on the National Health Service; Yuri Gagarin becomes the first man in space; construction of the Berlin Wall begins.

1962   The Cuban Missile Crisis takes place; the Telstar satellite transmits transatlantic TV; Nelson Mandela is jailed in South Africa; 'The Young Ones' by Cliff Richard is No 1.

1963   The Great Train Robbery takes place; President John F Kennedy is assassinated; Harold Wilson becomes Labour leader in the UK; the Profumo Affair causes a scandal.

1964   The UK sees £10 notes issued for the first time; BBC 2 comes to air with *Play School*; mods and rockers fight at seaside resorts in the UK; 'Can't Buy me Love' by the Beatles is released.

1965   Sir Winston Churchill dies; the Beatles are each awarded the Member of the Order of the British Empire; the United States bombs Vietnam; Edward Heath becomes leader of the Conservative Party; 'Goldie' the eagle escapes from London Zoo.

1966   London transport recruit staff from the West Indies; the Aberfan disaster shocks the world; England win football's World Cup; Harold Wilson announces a wage freeze; Walt Disney dies.

1967   Sir Francis Chichester sails around the world solo at the age of 65; the first heart transplant is performed; Torrey Canyon oil tanker disaster occurs; Sandie Shaw sings 'Puppet on a String' for the Eurovision Song Contest; Celtic win football's European Cup.

1968   Racing driver Jim Clark is killed in a race; Gary Sobers becomes the first man to hit six sixes in an over; Richard Nixon is elected US president.

1969   Prince Charles is invested as Prince of Wales; the 'troubles' flare up in Northern Ireland; 'The Eagle has landed' – Neil Armstrong is the first man on the moon; the Woodstock festival takes place.

Activity

Armchair shopping

You will need a selection of magazines for this activity. Write a list of 20 food items on a flip chart for all to see. Clients or teams then scan the magazines for a picture of each item to cut or tear out. Give them each a box or envelope to act as a shopping basket. The first to complete their shopping list, or the team who gathers the most items in a set time, wins. Afterwards, use the activity to discuss prices and how things have changed.

This week's excuse for a party!

Sixties night!

You might not get many takers for the dance floor and the disco might not be to everyone's taste, but then again you might just hit the right spot. There are plenty of 'sounds of the sixties' compilation CDs available, and it might be worth trying to set up a few disco lights to give some atmosphere. If people don't want to dance, you can play Name that Tune, a popular sixties quiz show. Try a range of sixties-type drinks such as Coca-Cola and Fanta. Beers such as Watneys Red Barrel or Double Diamond were popular, as were Babycham, snowballs and sweet white wine. For food, 'nibbles' were all the rage, such as cheese straws, sausage rolls, cocktail sausages, quiche, and cheese with pineapple on cocktail sticks. Create a sixties-inspired centrepiece by halving a grapefruit, covering it with silver foil and sticking the cheese and pineapple sticks into it. Glacé cherries on sticks were popular in drinks too. Crisps were also very popular and it was in the sixties that Golden Wonder introduced the new flavours of cheese and onion, smoky bacon, roast chicken and beef and onion. After the disco and quiz, have a classic sixties film at hand such as *The Sound of Music* or *Goldfinger*.

Week 9

February 26–March 4

Theme

Welsh food

The date 1 March is St David's Day, the patron saint of Wales. St David was an early saint who lived a frugal life, existing on herbs and bread and drinking only water. He is buried in St David's Cathedral, Pembroke. One of Wales' national emblems is a vegetable, the leek. It is said that St David ordered his soldiers to wear leeks in their caps. Leeks have long been a traditional ingredient in cawl, which is said to be the Welsh national dish.

Cawl

Cawl is a traditional stew or broth made from scraps of lamb, bits of bacon, cabbage and other vegetables. The recipes vary from place to place but essentially people would use whatever vegetables and scraps of meat they had to hand or were in season. Sometimes the broth is strained off and served as a starter followed by the meat and vegetables with some bread. One can easily imagine a large cauldron of this stewing on a fire in a cottage with the smell whetting everyone's appetites. The lamb is usually boiled on the bone the day before for an hour or so. This and the resulting stock is then added to the vegetables and bacon bits and stewed for about 2½ hours at 176°C. A whole head of chopped cabbage is added after an hour or so with a sprig of parsley.

Welsh rarebit (with sauce)

Welsh rarebit is essentially a form of cheese on toast. The cheese is usually cheddar and it is made into a sauce and poured over the bread. There are many possible variations regarding what is added to the cheese, but beer, mustard, pepper and Worcestershire sauce are common ingredients. To make enough for half a dozen people, warm ¼ pint milk and whisk in 1 tbsp flour, bring this to the boil and add 400 g grated cheddar. Melt the cheese and add 150 g breadcrumbs, 1 tsp Worcestershire sauce and 4 tbsp Guinness. Add some black pepper to taste and heat until it thickens. Pour the mixture over toast and grill it until it browns and bubbles. A quicker version is to mix 220 g grated cheddar, 25 g melted butter, 1 tsp Worcestershire sauce, 1 tsp mustard, 4 tbsp Guinness and a sprinkling of black pepper. Spread this on toast and grill. Serve with chutney and drink the rest of the Guinness!

Welsh cakes or griddle scones

Welsh cakes or griddle scones are a traditional teatime treat served with butter and jam. Rub 4 oz butter into 8 oz self-raising flour and then add 2 tbsp sultanas, 3 oz caster sugar and an egg. Form this into a dough, roll out the dough and cut it into circles. Grease a frying pan with butter and, when hot, 'fry' the cakes until golden brown and then flip each one over and brown the other side. Try adding a little grated lemon rind to the mix or a squeeze of lemon juice over the finished cakes.

FEB–MARCH

Activity

Welsh quiz

What is the highest mountain in Wales?

Snowdon

Spell Aberystwyth

A-b-e-r-y-s-t-w-y-t-h

Who wrote *Under Milk Wood*?

Dylan Thomas

What is the capital of Wales?

Cardiff

What is the Welsh name for Wales?

Cymru

What mythical creature is on the Welsh flag?

Dragon

What is an eisteddfod?

A festival of literature and music

Apart from a leek what is the other Welsh emblem?

Daffodil

From what is laver bread made?

Seaweed

Which 'Goon' was Welsh?

Harry Secombe

Who sang 'Big Spender'?

Dame Shirley Bassey

Who sang 'Green, Green Grass of Home'?

Tom Jones

Who won an Olympic gold medal for long jump in 1964?

Lynn Davies

Ray Reardon won which world championship six times in the 1970s?

Snooker

What river is the boundary between England and South Wales?

Severn

What colour is a Welsh poppy?

Yellow

Which Welsh-born author wrote *Charlie and the Chocolate Factory*?

Roald Dahl

What is the Welsh national anthem?

'Land of My Fathers'

When is the national day of Wales?

1 March

Which Welsh actor was married to Elizabeth Taylor?

Richard Burton

Activity

Choices and individuality

Individuality is important, especially in relation to food, as we all have our personal likes and dislikes. Key workers should find out what their clients' preferences are. Use friends and relatives if you can to add to the picture of favourite foods and drinks and preferred snacks, as well as favourite main meals. Also, what do they like for breakfast and when do they like to have it? What are their favourite biscuits and cakes? How often do they like to take a drink during the day? Do they like a nightcap? Do they like alcoholic drinks? There are many aspects of our clients' dietary habits that we ought to be better in touch with.

This week's excuse for a party!

Welsh night

Play some music by some famous Welsh singers such as Harry Secombe, Shirley Bassey, Katherine Jones and the male voice choirs singing songs such as 'Men of Harlech' and 'We'll Keep a Welcome'. Prepare some Welsh rarebit, have some Caerphilly cheese with biscuits to follow, and then do your Welsh quiz. Following this, settle down and watch a film about Wales such as *How Green was My Valley*, *Under Milk Wood*, *The Englishman Who Went Up a Hill But Came Down a Mountain* or *On The Black Hill*.

Week 10   ## March 5–11

Theme

Pancake Day

Pancake Day, or Shrove Tuesday, is a Christian festival falling on the Tuesday before Ash Wednesday, which is the first day of Lent. Lent used to be a period of strict fasting and contemplation but today people attempt to exercise self-discipline by giving up luxuries such as chocolate and alcohol. Fasting is common in many religions, as it is believed that suffering concentrates the mind on religious thoughts. The Anglo-Saxons were called to confession before Lent to be 'shriven' of their sins, hence the name 'Shrove' Tuesday. Shrove Tuesday then was a day when people prepared for the fast of Lent by using up all the eggs, milk and fat, which were not allowed in Lent … hence pancakes, which are the perfect way to use up these ingredients. It is said that the ingredients also have symbolic significance, eggs signifying creation; flour, the staff of life; and milk, purity. Others take the view that the pancakes represented a bit of a feast and a treat before the fast. The date varies from year to year but it is usually late February or early March. There are many recipe variations and ways to serve pancakes, so ask your clients for their recollections of Pancake Day and the different ways they ate pancakes. Here are a few ideas for pancakes.

Basic pancake

Put 100 g flour, a pinch of salt, 300 mL milk and two eggs into a bowl and whisk until lump-free. This is your 'batter' and should be left to stand for an hour. Melt some butter in a frying pan sufficient to cover the base and when the pan is very hot, pour in some batter. Fry the pancake until the underside is golden brown and then 'flip' it and 'brown' the other side. Serve the pancakes with sugar and lemon juice.

Alternative indulgence!

Serve a pancake spread with golden syrup and add a line of sliced banana and roll up the pancake. Then cover the top of the pancake with whipped cream. Also try the combination of strawberries in the middle and chocolate sauce on the top!

Savoury pancakes

Pancakes can be used not just for dessert but also for very good main courses too. One easy savoury version is to put mushrooms cooked in butter in the middle of the pancake, roll it up and cover the top with a cheese sauce.

Activity

Pancake Olympics!

Pancake races are traditional in the UK and date back to the 1400s. One school of thought has it that pancake races came about when a woman in Olney, Buckinghamshire, in 1445 was making pancakes when she heard the ringing of the 'shriving' bell and ran to the church still clutching her frying pan! During modern pancake races the pancake has to be tossed into the air and caught in the pan as you are running along. It might be difficult to organise a pancake race if you haven't got much room, but you can still hold a pancake tossing contest, whereby you see who can toss a pancake the most times in a minute!

Activity

Going to the pub

Many people used to visit their local pub or club on a regular basis to socialise, and for those clients who enjoy this it should be possible for them to visit their 'local'. The idea is to find a local where the clients will be welcome and where they will feel relaxed. They may play cards, darts, pool, or just chat and enjoy a drink or two and a bag of crisps. Many public bars have quiz nights, and some of the more traditional public houses still have a piano session occasionally. If your clients do not want to become 'regulars', then there is still the excuse to occasionally go out for a meal and a drink to a bar or restaurant. This provides an opportunity to get dressed up and feel good. You can get a menu beforehand so that people can choose what they would like to eat. Such trips can be expanded to include guests and relatives, and if enjoyed, any excuse should be used for a repeat performance. Similarly, within day centres, special days should be identified throughout the year for special meals at which formal dress is required.

This week's excuse for a party!

Pancake party

A pancake party is another opportunity to get people involved with preparation, serving and socialising. You will need a production line going if cooking on the night, but another option is you can precook the pancakes and reheat them in a hot oven so that everyone can be served at the same time. Have a range of different fillings and toppings available for people to try. Then sit down to let everyone digest and try this puzzle: How many words can you make from 'Pancake Day'? Have someone write the words down on a flip chart for all to see. Follow this puzzle with the following Pancake Olympic events.

Pancake balance

Have prepared thick corrugated cardboard pancakes about 30 cm in diameter. Each person then has a turn at walking across the room with a cardboard pancake balanced upon their head. This should raise a few laughs. If it is too easy, arrange a few obstacles along the course!

Pancake memory game

Use 12 pre-prepared cardboard pancakes. Stick a picture on one side of each cardboard pancake. The pictures should be 'pairs', with six pairs in all, so you might have two animals, two fruits, and so on. The cardboard pancakes are then shown around the group and then spread face down on the floor and shuffled around. Each taking a turn, the clients flip over two pancakes with a fish slice to try to find a pair. If the first person does not find a pair they are replaced and the next person has a go and so on until a pair is found. They are then replaced face down and the game starts again.

Week 11 March 12–18

Theme
Irish food

The date 17 March is St Patrick's Day. St Patrick, the patron saint of Ireland, was born in Scotland and kidnapped by Irish raiders at the age of 16 and put to work as a shepherd. He used the shamrock as a symbol to explain the Holy Trinity and is credited with driving snakes out of Ireland. As a way of stimulating reminiscence and discussion, ask your clients to draw up a list of all things Irish and write them down on a flip chart. Discuss your clients' experiences of visiting Ireland and any links they have with the country. Then move the discussion on to food by asking them to call out the names of Irish food and drinks. Irish food at its best is wholesome and simple. Potatoes feature heavily in the national diet, as in Irish stew, which could be called Ireland's national dish. The Irish are also famous for their soda bread and Guinness.

Irish stew

This is a crofter's meal traditionally made with just mutton, potatoes and onions. Many add carrots, but the truth is that life was hard for many poor peasants and they eked out a living using whatever came to hand or whatever was in season. Mutton was used because sheep were economically important for wool and milk – only the older animals ended up in the pot and so it needed to be cooked that bit longer to tenderise the meat. Take 2 lb mutton chopped into small pieces and put into a large pan with two large sliced onions and ¾ lb thickly sliced and halved potatoes. Add ¾ pint water, a sprig of parsley and salt and pepper to taste. Bring to the boil, cover and simmer for 2 hours. Add another ¾ lb potatoes and cook for another 40 minutes. This Irish stew can also be baked in an oven for 3 hours at 300°F. Serve the stew with soda bread.

Soda bread

Soda bread is a variety of bread where baking soda is the raising agent rather than yeast. Put 250 g plain flour, 250 g wholemeal flour, 1 tsp baking soda and 1 tsp salt into a bowl and mix well. Make a well in the middle and pour in 300 mL buttermilk and stir it again to make a soft, crumbly dough. Knead the dough for a few minutes and then shape it into flattened buns, dust with flour and cut a cross 2 cm deep on the top. Bake the bread at 200°C for about 30 minutes or so (until it sounds hollow when you tap it!).

Activity

Irish quiz (and an excuse for a sing-along)

What did St Patrick banish from Ireland?

Snakes

What is the capital of Eire?

Dublin

What is the famous illustrated eighteenth-century manuscript kept at Trinity College Dublin called?

The Book of Kells

What is Ireland's longest river called?

The River Shannon

What is the city of Waterford famous for?

Crystal

Goodbye Piccadilly, Farewell Leicester Square … where is it a long way to?

Tipperary

Spell leprechaun

L-e-p-r-e-c-h-a-u-n

What steals your heart away when they are smiling?

Irish eyes

Which stone will give you the gift of the gab if you kiss it?

The Blarney Stone

Who is the Irish wit, author and playwright who spent some time in Reading gaol for homosexuality and who famously said at customs, 'I have nothing to declare but my genius'?

Oscar Wilde

Who is the Irish author of *Gulliver's Travels*?

Jonathan Swift

Spell Guinness

G-u-i-n-n-e-s-s

In Dublin's fair city, where the girls are so pretty, I first set my eyes on sweet … who?

Molly Malone

For whom are the pipes calling?

Danny Boy

Who will you take home again?

Kathleen

What is the national game of some violence and played with a wooden stick?

Hurling

Traditional Irish bread is called what?

Soda bread

What is a ceilidh (pronounced kaylee)?

A dance (give a bonus point for spelling it)

Where, at the closing of the day, might you sit and watch the sun go down?

Galway Bay

Which Irish poet's epitaph reads, 'Cast a cold Eye / On Life, on Death. / Horseman, pass by.'

WB Yeats

This week's excuse for a party!

Irish night

This week's party will provide you with an excuse for making Irish-themed decorations and then decorating the room and table ready for the 'session'! Have some Irish sing-along CDs prepared too, as there are many well-known Irish songs. The food will of course be the Irish stew with your own soda bread. For dessert have a group make basic cupcakes and then have them decorate the cupcakes in the traditional Irish colours of green, white and orange. Use coloured icing and green and orange food colouring to make a 'lurid' plate of themed cakes! The second part of the evening is a Guinness tasting session to let all try out the flavour of Guinness. Also have some other Irish drinks on offer, such as Baileys Irish Cream and some Irish whisky, and of course some tea for those who don't like alcoholic drinks. You can also try your hand at making some Irish coffee, which is a fresh coffee with some brown sugar and a dram of whisky and topped with some thick cream. Alternatively, try coffee with Baileys. The entertainment can be your Irish quiz and then you can settle down to watch a film about Ireland such as *Waking Ned*, a very funny comedy, or *The Quiet Man*, a film from 1952 starring John Wayne.

Week 12 March 19–25

Theme

Mother's Day and Europe

Mother's Day is traditionally the fourth Sunday of Lent in the UK (Mothering Sunday), but Mother's Day is celebrated around the world in different ways and at different times, with many countries (eg the United States) celebrating it in May. The day is usually marked by children giving cards, flowers and presents to their mothers and either taking them for a special meal or baking them a special cake. Traditionally, it was a day when daughters who had gone to work in 'service' as domestic servants were given a day off to visit their mothers. There is much to share about clients' own mothers and their experiences of motherhood. What did they call their mother? Was it Ma, Mom, Mum or Mama? Ask about how they used to celebrate Mother's Day. This conversation can lead on to discussing the trials and tribulations of motherhood and how the role of the mother or 'housewife' has changed over the years. Here are a few sayings that will help to stimulate discussion and recall.

Mother knows best.
A man loves his wife the best but his mother the longest!
God can't be everywhere so he created mothers.
A mother understands what a child doesn't say.

The food item specially associated with Mothering Sunday is the Simnel cake, which is a fruit cake with two layers of almond paste, one on top and one in the middle. The name is believed to come from a brother and sister, Simon and Nell: they wanted to make a cake for their mother but one thought it should be baked and the other wanted to boil it, so in the end they did both, hence sim-nel. The cake signifies the end of Lent and so it is rich in things that were not allowed during the fast, such as fruit and spices, and it is also traditionally eaten at Easter too. The cake is made with 11 balls of marzipan icing on top, representing Jesus' disciples minus Judas.

Simnel cake

Take 300 g self-raising flour and rub 110 g butter or margarine into it. Add to this 100 g brown sugar, 350 g mixed dried fruit, a pinch of salt and ½ tsp mixed spice and stir it all up. Next, add 3 tbsp golden syrup and two eggs and continue to stir it, adding about 100mL of milk to create a soft mix. Grease a large baking cake tin and put half the mixture in and cover that with a layer of rolled-out marzipan. Add the rest of the mixture to the cake tin and bake it at around 150°C for 1¼ hours. When baked, allow the cake to cool and then paint it with a thick paste of water and icing sugar. Cover this paste with a layer of marzipan and pattern the edges with a fork. Place 11 marzipan balls, rolled in icing sugar, on the top of the cake, around the edge. You can then decorate the centre however you wish.

Activity

Europe and European food quiz

The date 25 March also marks the day the European Economic Community was established in 1957. There is still controversy among nations as to whether they should belong to the European Economic Community or not. Before the Europe and European food quiz, hold a quick discussion about whether people think we should or should not stay in the European Economic Community, and then hold a quick poll. Start your quiz before the debate gets too heated!

What Italian city gives its name to a type of ham?

Parma

Where does Emmenthal cheese come from?

Switzerland

Feta cheese comes from where?

Greece

What was created by French monks to look like a child's arms folded in prayer?

The pretzel

Spell the traditional French fish stew 'bouillabaisse'

B-o-u-i-l-l-a-b-a-i-s-s-e

Which country gives us soda bread?

Ireland

Sheep offal encased in a sheep's stomach would be what?

Haggis

Where did chips originate?

Belgium

What country is the pasta and pizza capital of the world?

Italy

Who eats l'escargot, or snails?

The French

Where are you likely to come across paella?

Spain

Where does pumpernickel originate?

Germany

What country gives us Gouda cheese?

The Netherlands

What country gives us the 'green wine' vinho verde?

Portugal

Where would you be if you had dolmades followed by ouzo?

Greece

What country is famous for its chocolates and beers?

Belgium

If you were enjoying a 'bigos' where would you be?

Poland

Where did doner kebabs originate?

Turkey

What country gave us goulash?

Hungary

In what country would you eat laver bread?

Wales

Activity

Kitchen tidy

This craft idea takes a terracotta flowerpot and decorates it to make an attractive holder for kitchen utensils. There are several variations you can try, including covering the pot with a découpage of flowers or similar in a colour to suit your kitchen colour scheme, or to leave the terracotta background and découpage a few real autumn leaves onto it for a nice effect. You then varnish the pot to make it last and give it a nice sheen. The idea can also be used to make some interesting plant pots for indoor use.

Speechmark

This week's excuse for a party!

Lady's night!

A simnel cake can be prepared along with a range of other treats and a buffet. The twist is that it is all to be prepared and made by the men in the group, who must also decorate the room with flowers and wait upon the ladies and serve the drinks. The assembled company can then dance the night away to music as requested by the ladies beforehand or watch a film of the ladies' choice. Some good films celebrating womanhood are *Nine to Five*, *The King and I* and *Tea with Mussolini*.

Week 13   March 26 – April 1

Theme

The seventies, fast food and disco!

The 1970s saw the UK joining the Common Market and strikes resulting in power cuts and food shortages. This got so bad that the 1978/1979 winter was called the Winter of Discontent, in stark contrast to the fashions and glitz of the era's disco craze and the film *Saturday Night Fever* with the aptly named Bee Gees hit song 'Stayin' Alive'!

The seventies also gave us spacehoppers and the 'great smell of' Brut, with boxing legend Henry Cooper inviting us to 'splash it all over'! There were also strange emerging styles and trends in food ideas and flavours. Marketing was becoming increasingly clever and humorous with such campaigns as the Martian robots advertising Smash instant potatoes, who couldn't stop laughing at the way humans peel, slice and boil potatoes and then 'smash them all to pieces'! Pizza was becoming increasingly popular as a fast food, and snack pots and pot noodles appeared on the scene. Can you also remember such seventies food delights as the Curly Wurly and Monster Munch? Television cookery shows included Graham Kerr's *The Galloping Gourmet*. He was famous for drinking copious amounts of wine while cooking. There was also Delia Smith with her cookery show *Family Fare*. The phrase 'couch potato' was coined in the United States, referring to people spending their free time lying on the sofa watching TV and eating junk food. In general, fewer fruits and vegetables were being eaten with the continuing rise of convenience foods such as ready-made lasagne and fish fingers. The number of supermarkets grew, and by the end of the decade almost half the population had freezers and were doing one big weekly shop instead of topping up frequently at the local grocers. Dinner parties were increasingly popular with the likes of hostess trolleys and soda siphons. They were often informal disco-type events with the food becoming more of a sideline, often being a help-yourself buffet with a wide selection of sweet and savoury items. The basic mix was prawn cocktails, cheese straws, cocktail sausages, quiche, celery sticks, vol-au-vents, crisps and nuts.

Celery sticks

Cut celery into short sections. Fill the celery hollow with cream cheese and dust with paprika. Try some with mashed tuna and some with peanut butter!

Prawn cocktail

Line some glass cocktail dishes or large wine glasses with lettuce leaves. Dice some cucumber into the bottom. Make a paste of mayonnaise and tomato purée or ketchup (1 tsp purée to ¼ pint mayonnaise). Take some defrosted, peeled and cooked prawns and add them to the mayonnaise and tomato mixture and combine. Dollop the mixture on top of the cucumber and then dust each prawn cocktail with paprika.

Mushroom vol-au-vents

Cook some ready-made vol-au-vent cases. Fry some chopped mushrooms in butter and stir into this a white sauce mix, adding a little salt and pepper to taste. Bring to the boil, allow to cool and then spoon into the cases. Try other fillings such as cream with a strawberry on top, cream cheese, egg mayonnaise and cress, or feta cheese and olives.

Discussion activity
Some notable events of the 1970s

1970 Remember the Raleigh Chopper? This child's bicycle was introduced this year. The year 1970 sees the Isle of Wight Festival, where you can see Jimi Hendrix and the Who, among many others, for £3; the Beatles split up.

1971 Decimal coins are introduced; 'hot pants' are in fashion; Clackers are all the rage but the toy is banned by some schools; *The French Connection* was a popular film.

1972 Oxford admits female students; the Munich Olympics are marred by terrorists; David Bowie becomes Ziggy Stardust; 'Bloody Sunday' occurs in Northern Ireland. The film *The Godfather* was released.

1973 A nationwide coal miners' strike leads to a 3-day working week in Great Britain; Roger Moore becomes James Bond in the film *Live and Let Die*; Princess Anne marries Mark Philips; *Last of the Summer Wine* series begins on TV.

1974 President Nixon resigns because of the Watergate scandal; Abba win the Eurovision Song Contest with 'Waterloo'; McDonald's comes to London.

1975 The Vietnam War ends; the Sex Pistols and punk music arrive; *Jaws* comes to the cinema screen; Muhammad Ali beats Joe Frazier in the 'Thrilla in Manila'; Spain becomes a democracy after dictator Francisco Franco's death.

1976 Mao Tse-tung dies; riots occur in Soweto, South Africa; Concorde comes into service; Ford launch the Fiesta; Harold Wilson resigns as prime minister of the UK.

1977 This is the Queen's Silver Jubilee year; Elvis Presley dies; over a million skateboards are sold in the UK; the film *Star Wars* is released.

1978 The Yorkshire Ripper is at large; Ian Botham became a cricketting hero; the Bee Gees are top of the pops with 'Stayin' Alive', as were Boney M with 'Rivers of Babylon'.

1979 Margaret Thatcher becomes Britain's first female prime minister; the game Trivial Pursuit is invented; the price of milk rises to 15p a pint (today it is around 70p) ; Sebastian Coe sets a new mile record of 3 minutes and 48.95 seconds; the Vauxhall Astra is launched.

Activity

Food and drink quotations for discussion

We live in an age when pizza gets to your home before the police.
Jeff Marder

Things that are said to do you good generally taste of sawdust or burnt rubber.
R Howarth

He who does not mind his belly, will hardly mind anything else.
Samuel Johnson

I'm like an old wine. They don't bring me out very often, but I'm well preserved.

Rose F Kennedy (on her 100th birthday)

My mother's menu consisted of two choices:
Take it or leave it.

Buddy Hackett

One cannot think well, love well, sleep well, if one has not dined well.

Virginia Woolf

Man is what he eats.

Ludwig Feuerbach

The belly rules the mind.

Spanish proverb

This week's excuse for a party!

Seventies night dinner party

No cooking on the night, just lots of finger foods and your celery sticks, vol-au-vents and prawn cocktails. Don't forget the box of Milk Trays and the Walnut Whips, two seventies favourites. Popular contemporary drinks were sweet white German wines such as a Riesling like Blue Nun, rosé wines such as Mateus Rosé, Cinzano and 'anytime, anyplace, anywhere it's ... Martini'. Foreign holidays had also made bottles of Chianti in wicker baskets popular. Apart from disco, Trivial Pursuit was popular, so it would be good to organise this as a quiz for the evening. There are many seventies-themed CDs available to play as background music or to dance to or, once again, play Name that Tune. Afterwards, you might like to watch the seventies classic *Saturday Night Fever*, as this will bring back some memories about what we used to wear and the music we used to listen to. The other classic that will probably make you cringe to watch again is the play *Abigail's Party* – this has a wonderful seventies soundtrack but it is also a fascinating cameo of adult social morals of the decade.

Week 14 April 2–8

Theme

Easter

Easter holds deep religious significance for many, representing the resurrection of Christ and symbolising new beginnings. Most of us as children looked forward to the Easter holidays and to the Easter eggs too, of course. There are many foods associated with Easter but chocolate eggs are the most significant. The egg signifies new life, and the tradition of giving eggs dates back to pagan times and celebrating the coming of spring. Hot cross buns are another traditional Easter treat that again date back to pre-Christian times, with the bun symbolising the moon and the cross representing the moon's four quarters. A variety of cakes were baked for Easter, including the simnel cake, which we explored on Mother's Day in Week 12, but another was the chocolate cake, which you could bake and decorate for Easter!

Chocolate cake

This recipe comes from a popular *Be-Ro Home Recipes* book from 1957. Beat 2 oz sugar and 2 oz margarine into a cream. Stir in 4 oz flour with 2 tsp cocoa and a few drops of vanilla essence along with a beaten mix of an egg and 2 tbsp milk. Mix thoroughly and pour into a greased cake tin and bake at 350°F for 30 minutes. The chocolate icing was 2 tbsp icing sugar and 2 tbsp cocoa mixed to a smooth paste with water and a few drops of vanilla essence. After baking the cake and icing it, your clients can then get creative with the Easter-themed decoration.

An alternative recipe, from the thirty-sixth edition of *Foulsham's Universal Cookery Book* (first published around 1930), merely gives you the following:

Take ¼ lb chocolate powder, ½ lb flour, 6 oz margarine, 6 oz castor sugar, 4 tbsp milk, 2 eggs and ¼ tsp bicarbonate of soda and mix all together adding beaten eggs and milk last. Bake in hot oven and coat with chocolate icing.

Activity
DIY egg decorating

Buy some inexpensive Easter eggs and decorate them with cake-decorating materials. You can get tubes of coloured icing to write messages and you can use 'blobs' of icing to stick sweets and edible decorations onto the eggs.

Activity
Quick cookery quiz

What does julienne mean?
Cut into thin strips

What does parboil mean?
Partially boiled

What does 'au gratin' mean?
Topped with breadcrumbs or grated cheese

What is chowder?
Soup

The spice saffron is made from which flower?
Crocus

What is a sauce thickening made from flour and butter?
A roux

What is the main ingredient of a risotto?
Rice

What herb is used to make a pesto sauce?
Basil

If something is 'à la lyonnaise' it is cooked with what?
Onions

What do you call beef cooked in pastry?
Beef Wellington

What pasta is named after little worms?
Vermicelli

What is a Moroccan cooking pot called?
A tagine

What fish produces caviar?
The sturgeon

Mixed with onion, what herb is commonly used for stuffing?
Sage

What flavour does fennel have?
Aniseed

What food is literally called 'fly with the wind'?
Vol-au-vent

What is the hottest Indian curry?
Phall

Baklava is made with what sort of pastry?
Filo

What nut is praline made from?
Almond

What is a courgette called in the United States?
A zucchini

Activity

Cooking

Cooking is an essential part of normal life, and getting some clients to prepare a meal for themselves occasionally is an excellent way of rekindling old skills and making people feel useful and involved. A meal involves many functions in its preparation and delivery. Clients will have to plan what to have, organise the shopping, cook it, lay the tables, chill the wine, and so forth. Alas, there is the clearing-away and the washing-up to do too. Such activity should be a regular weekly event for those who are capable, as it gives back responsibility and control. For those in residential settings, inviting friends and relatives to join them can heighten the importance of the meal. Individual clients could have their family to private meals in their rooms. There is also no reason why clients should not be involved in the kitchens generally, and certainly they should be making simple snacks for themselves such as beans on toast, where this is desirable.

This week's excuse for a party!

Easter-lympics!

Age is no barrier to having fun and this week's party is based simply upon having some fun. There are many activities you can undertake that might at first appear to be childish, but it is the way you undergo these activities that renders them inoffensive and age appropriate. So bring out all the cakes you have made and have a tea party with the clients' favourite sandwiches. Follow this with these three games to get people socialising and laughing.

Egg-and-spoon race

Use chocolate Easter eggs on spoons and carry these around a circuit of the room and over obstacles. Drop the egg and you are back to the start.

Hunt the egg

Unknown to the clients you have secreted a dozen small Easter eggs around the room that must now be found.

Egg bowling

Eggs are oval shaped and therefore do not roll in a straight line, so egg bowling is great fun to play and watch. You can play it like tenpin bowling, with tubes of sweets to knock down, or like bowls, with a small egg as the jack and cream eggs to roll.

Week 15
April 9–15

Theme

Diets and healthy eating

Diets and healthy eating are themes close to our hearts and can cause some consternation as we realise that what we like is often not good for us. Most of us have tried to give something up or have tried to alter our diet in an effort to lose some weight or get fitter, and such attempts can be explored. Have some pictures or samples of diet foods and dieting products to pass around the group to stimulate discussion. Ask if anyone tried clubs such as Weight Watchers or joined gyms in order to lose weight. Ask the group if, in general, people are more concerned for their appearance than their health, as for many young people these days dieting is an aid to gaining 'the perfect figure'! Are teenagers today too thin? Have some contrasting pictures of forties and modern pin-ups to compare. Here are some healthy(ish) options.

Chicken kebab

Drain a tin of pineapple chunks. To the pineapple juice add 2 tbsp brown sugar, ⅓ cup sherry, ¼ cup soy sauce, a pinch of ground ginger and a pinch of garlic powder. Cut some chicken breasts into small cubes and place these in the marinade with the pineapple chunks and leave in the refrigerator for 2 hours, stirring occasionally. Drain these and thread alternately onto skewers and grill for around 20 minutes under a medium-hot grill, rotating the kebabs every now and again.

Orange and carrot muffins

Mix 330 g flour, 2 tsp baking powder, the zest of two oranges, 100 g caster sugar and ½ tsp cinnamon together thoroughly with a pinch of salt. In another bowl, whisk an egg, the juice of two oranges and 75 g butter together and add 100 g grated carrots. Add this wet mixture to the dry mixture and combine. Spoon the mixture into muffin tins and bake for around 25 minutes at 80°C.

Fruit kebabs

Impale chunks of banana, strawberry, pineapple and orange on bamboo skewers. Heat 300 mL single cream, 1 tsp orange zest and 1 tbsp freshly squeezed orange juice. When boiling, reduce heat and add 250 g plain dark chocolate chunks, stirring the liquid until the chocolate is melted and blended in. Decant the liquid into a bowl and dip the fruit kebabs into it and eat immediately. For a slightly different version, you could use milk chocolate for a less healthy option or you could add an orange liqueur to the dip.

Activity

Diet discussion

Ask your local dietician to come and lead a session, and back this up with lots of leaflets. The theme of the discussion is 'What is a healthy diet?' – what is good for us and what is not? How can we make sure we get adequate protein, vitamins, minerals, fats and carbohydrates and what foods contain what? You can also discuss the merits of common healthy eating advice that states the following points.

- Base meals on starchy food. These foods include potatoes, rice, pasta and cereals. These carbohydrates contain fibre and fill you up and give you longer-lasting energy than sugars.

- Eat lots of fruit and vegetables. Five a day will give you lots of vitamins, minerals and more fibre.

- Eat more fish. A good source of protein with useful vitamin, minerals and omega-3 fatty acids, which are good for the brain.

- Eat less saturated fat and sugar. This reduces your cholesterol and keeps blood pressure down, reducing the risk of heart disease and stroke. Reducing sugar will help you lose weight and will be good for your teeth and gums.

- Eat less salt. This helps reduce blood pressure.

- Take more exercise. This helps you burn calories and lose weight, is good for your heart and helps reduce blood pressure.

- Keep well hydrated. Drink at least 1.2 L a day, and more when you are active or when it is warm.

This week's excuse for a party!

A healthy weight-watchers party!

Take a group trip around the local supermarket looking for low-fat, healthy party food options to supplement your muffins and kebabs. As a centrepiece take some dishes and fill them with a selection of low-fat cheeses, such as spreadable cheese and cottage cheese. Into these dishes stand celery, carrot, red pepper and cucumber sticks and sprinkle finely grated carrot over it. Try one with low-fat peanut butter too.

Also, try the following easy-to-make healthy drinks.

Banana and chocolate smoothie

Take 2 tbsp low-calorie chocolate drink powder, four ice cubes, a large banana and 300 mL skimmed milk and blend it.

Limeade

Blend a dozen limes complete with skin, 200 g caster sugar and 100 mL water. Sift out the bits and pour the liquid into a jug with lots of ice. Check for sourness and add more sugar if it is too sour. Top it up with some soda water and float some lime slices on the top.

Raspberryade

Place 300 g caster sugar, a sliced lemon, a sliced orange, 350 mL water and about 500 g raspberries in a saucepan and bring to the boil. When the liquid is cool, sieve it. Pour it into a jug, cool in the refrigerator and mix with 50 per cent soda water to serve.

Week 16   April 16–22

Theme

Sweets

The sweets from our childhood and school days are well embedded in our memories and you would not be alone in admitting that you used to spend your dinner money at the local sweet shop on the way to school. A list of some sweets of yesteryear will suffice to get clients started on what their particular favourites were. Fruit gums, Smarties, Spangles, Arrow bars, Milkybars, sweet cigarettes, Curly Wurlys, Lucky Bags, bubble gum, liquorice allsorts, gobstoppers, sherbet dips, flying saucers, Spanish (liquorice), Fry's chocolate cream bar, Walnut Whips, Love Hearts, Parma Violets, aniseed balls, army and navy sweets, Refreshers, Black Jack Chews, rhubarb and custard drops, lollies, shrimps and chocolate mice, to name just a few!

You can't possibly reminisce about sweets without having some samples to stimulate the taste buds and rekindle the experience. So visit your local sweet shop to get prepared for this session. If you can't find what you want, try these websites, which have many of the old favourites.

* www.aquarterof.co.uk
* www.sweetandnostalgic.co.uk
* www.woolworthsmuseum.co.uk

When you have finished reminiscing about these, have a go at making some sweets with the following simple recipes.

Peppermint creams

Mix together 300 g sugar, one egg white and some peppermint flavouring to form a stiff paste. Cut the mixture into shapes and put it in the fridge to cool. That's all there is to it! Experiment with this recipe by using different flavourings such as adding freshly squeezed orange juice or cocoa powder and maybe some orange rind or lemon zest. Check cookery magazines for other recipes, or get a book from the library and set up a sweet-making group.

Orange chocolates

Mix together 120 g icing sugar and 75 g cocoa powder and then thoroughly mix this with 100 g unsalted butter. Mix in 75 g finely chopped orange zest and press it into a shallow tray. Leave the chocolate to set and then chop it into sweet-sized pieces. As an alternative flavour you could add 75 g chopped almonds or 2 tbsp strong coffee.

Coconut ice

Mix 100 g condensed milk with 200 g desiccated coconut and 500 g icing sugar. Press half of the mixture into a shallow non-stick tin. Mix some pink food colouring to the rest of the mixture and then spread it over the top of the first layer. Place the coconut ice in the refrigerator to set and then cut it into bite-sized squares.

Activity

Cryptic sweets quiz

A posh road
Quality Street

Have a break have a …
Kit Kat

Mutinous coconut
Bounty

Clever sweets
Smarties

Wobbly infants
Jelly babies

Gambler's sweet
Black Jack

Given to keep someone quiet
Gobstopper

In the middle of room and moor
M&M

Alfresco chocolate bar
Picnic

Mother's local pub
Mars bar

Toothless Chardonnay
Wine gum

For sporty royals and Marco
Polo

Noisy beetle or Scrooge's favourite sweet
Humbug

Assorted girls
Dolly mixtures

Istanbul harem
Turkish Delight

Scottish capital granite
Edinburgh rock

And all because the lady loves …
Milk Tray

Voodoo chocolates
Black Magic

Too good to hurry
Murray Mints

Policemen
Kop Kops

This week's excuse for a party!

Sweet games night

An after-dinner evening of games using sweets will be a great social event where it will be difficult not to eat all your winnings. 'I'll see your three aniseed balls and raise you two chocolate buttons'!

After this frantic burst of energy and sweet munching, what could be better than to sit down and watch the post-party film, which of course will have to be Willy Wonka & the Chocolate Factory.

Pontoon

Play the card game Pontoon around the table, using small sweets or chocolate buttons as substitute coins.

Poker

Poker is a game for the serious card sharps. Here is the order of hands from best to worst.

- Royal flush: A, K, Q, J, 10 of same suit
- Straight flush: five cards of the same suit in sequence
- Four of a kind: four cards of the same rank and any one other card
- Full house: three cards of one rank and two of another
- Flush: five cards of the same suit
- Straight: five cards, mixed suits, in sequence (eg 4, 5, 6, 7, 8)
- Three of a kind: three cards of the same rank
- Two pair: two cards of one rank and two cards of another
- One pair: two cards of the same rank

Bingo

Play bingo but using sweets to cover the numbers instead of a pen.

Sweet price guess

Have a selection of sweets to hand in their wrappers and divide the group into teams. Hold up each item and get the group to guess what they cost. The team that guesses closest to the cost gets the sweet.

Pass the Polo

To play Pass the Polo, form two lines of people where each person has a straw in their mouth. The two teams race each other to pass the Polo from straw to straw (no hands), from one end of the line to the other. Dropped polos go back to the start!

Memory tray

This is a good version of the memory game. Place 20 different sweets on a tray and cover the tray. Uncover the tray for 20 seconds to allow the clients to see the sweets and then recover the tray. Ask the clients to list all of the sweets they remember seeing on the tray.

How many?

Another easy guessing game is to try to guess the number of sweets in a packet.

Week 17 April 23–29

Theme

English food

The date 23 April is St George's Day, so our focus this week is upon English cuisine. St George, incidentally, wasn't actually English. It is thought that St George was a Roman soldier who protested against the Romans' torture of Christians and who died for his beliefs. The legend of St George's fight with a dragon was brought back to Europe by the Crusaders, and it is suggested that the dragon is a representation of the devil from which St George is saving the maid.

Just what is the national dish of England though? Get the clients to write suggestions on a flip chart. There will be many contenders, including the traditional Sunday lunch favourite of roast beef with Yorkshire pudding. Others will cite the traditional English breakfast – or 'Full Monty', as it is also known. There are also regional specialities such as Cornish pasties and Lancashire hotpot and many other favourites such as bangers and mash, ploughman's lunch, shepherd's pie, toad-in-the-hole and not forgetting of course, fish and chips. Others will point to the great British sandwich, which the Earl of Sandwich devised in the eighteenth century so that he could eat without having to leave the gambling tables. Many will point out that we now live in a multicultural society and the most popular food in many polls is in fact the curry 'chicken tikka masala'! This is not such a modern phenomenon, because the first Indian restaurant opened in London in around 1809! Another good contender for England's national dish could be 'anything on toast', and of course we cannot forget the phenomenon we call 'afternoon tea', with its cakes, scones and jam!

APRIL

Yorkshire pudding

Yorkshire pudding can be a main meal or a dessert. The perfect Yorkshire pudding is a thing of legend and is not so easy to master. It is basically the same mixture as pancakes, with flour and eggs, and it is traditionally cooked in a large shallow tin and then cut into squares. Modern supermarket versions tend to be small, light and fluffy, whereas it was meant to be quite a substantial source of food, often acting as the major part of a meal in the absence of meat. Cover the bottom of a large, flat roasting tin with vegetable oil and place in an oven at 220°C. Whisk two large eggs with 200 mL milk. Add two pinches of salt and 100 g flour and whisk it all together. Take the tin out of the oven and carefully pour the batter onto the hot oil, tipping the tin so that the batter spreads evenly. Return the tin to the oven and bake the batter until the pudding rises and browns. This will be delicious served on its own with an onion gravy, but also try the sweet version, pouring golden syrup over the Yorkshire pudding with a sprinkling of sugar – delicious.

National drink!

Trying to agree upon England's national drink is equally as difficult as agreeing upon the national dish, so ask the clients to decide whether it is tea, gin and tonic, spring water, beer, Pimm's, mead, sherry, milk, orange juice or have we become a nation of fizzy drink lovers. If we had to decide upon the drink that best represents England, what would it be? One final question to ponder with respect to tea … is it milk first or tea first?

Activity

English quiz

Where was William Shakespeare born?

Stratford-upon-Avon

What waterways are Norfolk famous for?

The Broads

Which two universities compete in the annual 'Boat Race'?

Oxford and Cambridge

Where are The Lawn Tennis Championships held?

Wimbledon

Which city has a famous commercial area called the 'Bullring'?

Birmingham

Who hid from the Sheriff of Nottingham in Sherwood Forest with his Merry Men and Maid Marian?

Robin Hood

Where will you find the 'Crown Jewels'?

The Tower of London

In what county is John Constable's *The Hay Wain* set?

Suffolk

Where is the home of the 'Red Devils' and *Coronation Street*?

Manchester

Where do Druids worship the sun in a circle of large stones?

Stonehenge

What is the highest mountain in England?

Scafell Pike

Where are the Potteries?

Stoke-on-Trent

Where do bluebirds fly over white cliffs according to the song?

Dover

Where did William the Conqueror defeat King Harold?

Hastings

Where is the home of the Beatles?

Liverpool

What is the name of the Queen's principle residence?

Buckingham Palace

Where was St Thomas Becket murdered and to where do pilgrims progress?

Canterbury

What is the big bell of the clock at the Houses of Parliament called?

Big Ben

What northern seaside town is famous for its tower and illuminations?

Blackpool

Who is the greatest English man or woman who ever lived?

(There is not right or wrong answer, but this question will provoke much discussion)

This week's excuse for a party!

St George's night party

What could be better than to have a quintessentially English afternoon tea? Make a selection of the clients' favourite sandwiches, not forgetting cucumber sandwiches with the crusts removed! Also, have a selection of cupcakes alongside some scones with strawberry jam and clotted cream. The tea should be served in teapots covered with tea cosies, the milk in little jugs and the sugar in bowls. Apart from tea, have some Pimm's for people to try or a glass of sherry to whet the appetite. Play some light classical English music such as *Elizabethan Serenade*, *Fantasia on Greensleeves*, *The Lark Ascending* or Percy Grainger's 'Country Gardens'. Hold an English quiz and then sit back to watch any one of many films about England or the English, such as *Oliver!*, *The Lady Vanishes*, *Great Expectations*, *Saturday Night and Sunday Morning* or one of the 'Carry On' series of comedies.

Week 18 April 30–May 6

Theme

The 1980s

The 1980s were a decade of politics, with the Falklands War and high unemployment. The global AIDS epidemic was coming to light, and in Britain a royal wedding added some much-needed relief to the decade. The eighties started with the 1978/1979 Winter of Discontent, the miners' strike, food shortages and power cuts. On the health front, there was a craze for fitness videos such as *Jane Fonda's Workout* and in 1984 the London Marathon was run for the first time. Video games became popular and the decade's favourite toys included My Little Pony and the Rubik's cube, alongside a multitude of Star Wars-themed toys. Musically, we had Live Aid and 'New Romantics' such as Duran Duran, Boy George and Adam and the Ants. Fashions included the 'mullet' hairstyle, shoulder pads, headbands and leggings. On the food front, convenience foods and 'ready meals' were developing fast. Microwave ovens gave us meals in minutes and we saw the introduction of many new forms of easy-to-cook processed foods and ready-cooked frozen meals. This was somewhat at odds with the TV cookery shows of the decade. *Madhur Jaffrey's Indian Cookery* programme was trying to get us to explore spices, and Anton Mosimann was extolling the virtues of 'nouvelle cuisine', where the emphasis was on lighter cooking and fancy presentation – it was cynically called 'posh nosh'! We also had *Ken Hom's Chinese Cookery*, causing a big surge in wok sales. Health concerns helped pasta to become popular and supermarkets were trying to get us to try different foods such as spaghetti bolognese, which became a dinner party favourite, washed down with supermarket Beaujolais. Cheesecake was a popular dessert at such parties. Health concerns also fuelled the F-plan diet, F standing for fibre and the idea being that you fill up on low-fat, high-fibre fruit and vegetables, including potatoes, and pasta. Shopping-wise, we were introduced to barcodes, widgets in beer cans, low-fat margarines and Twiglets! Children were catered for with such sweet delights as Cherry Lips, Fizzy Cola Bottles, Wispa bars, Caramac, Drumsticks and Space Dust!

Cheesecake

Crush 4 oz digestive biscuits and mix in 2 oz melted butter. Tamp this down into the bottom of a cake tin. Mix 2 oz caster sugar with 8 oz cream cheese and then add to this two beaten eggs and the rind and juice from one lemon. Pour it over the biscuit base and bake at 250°F for around 45 minutes. When the cheesecake is cold, decorate with strawberries or mandarin segments, or any way you like.

Discussion activity

Some notable events of the 1980s

1980   Ronald Reagan is elected president of the United States; John Lennon is shot dead; Björn Borg wins Wimbledon for the fifth year running.

1981   Prince Charles marries Lady Diana Spencer; Ken Barlow marries Deirdre Langton in *Coronation Street*; the first London Marathon is run; we have the Greenham Common Women's Peace Camp, the Indiana Jones film *Raiders of the Lost Ark* is released; Roger Moore is James Bond in *For Your Eyes Only*.

1982   The Falklands War is fought; the compact disc arrives on the scene; Michael Jackson releases the album *Thriller*; the film *E.T. the Extra-Terrestrial* is released; the Ford Sierra is launched, replacing the Cortina.

1983   Madonna becomes very popular; this year also sees *Star Wars: Episode VI – Return of the Jedi*; *Auf Wiedersehen, Pet* is a popular TV series; Lech Wałesa wins the Nobel Peace Prize.

1984   The Apple Macintosh personal computer is introduced; the miners' strike begins in the UK; the first 'untethered' spacewalk takes place!

1985   Live Aid is held; *EastEnders* is first broadcast; Bradford City stadium and Heysel Stadium football disasters occur; the wreck of the *RMS Titanic* is located.

1986   Prince Andrew marries Sarah Ferguson; Diego Maradona's 'Hand of God' goal knocks England out of the 1986 FIFA World Cup; Newcastle's Metrocentre shopping centre opens; the M25 is finished.

1987   The cross-channel ferry *SS Herald of Free Enterprise* sinks, killing 200; bad October storms in the UK kill 23; Margaret Thatcher is re-elected for a third term; the Channel Tunnel gets the go-ahead; Kylie Minogue releases 'I Should be so Lucky'.

1988   The Lockerbie air disaster occurs when a jumbo jet is blown up by terrorists, killing 270; Liverpool wins their sixth English Football League Championship this decade; the first Comic Relief 'Red Nose Day' is held.

1989   The Berlin Wall falls; Robin Day chairs Question Time for
the last time and the BBC's *Breakfast News* is aired for the
first time; Wallace and Gromit arrive on the scene with the
film *A Grand Day Out*.

Activity

The poetry of food and drink

There are a few poems concerning food and drink, most of them
humorous, and they form the basis of an interesting read-and-discuss
group. Here are some suggestions of poems to look up.

- 'Address to a Haggis', by Robert Burns
- 'Apples', by Laurie Lee
- 'To a Goose', by Robert Southey
- 'The Gourmet's Love Song', by PG Wodehouse
- 'A Drinking Song', by WB Yeats
- 'Little Red Riding Hood and the Wolf', by Roald Dahl
- 'Mutton', by Jonathan Swift

Finally, one by that famous poet Anon:

If all the land were apple pie,
And all the sea were ink;
And all the trees were bread and cheese,
What should we do for drink?

This week's excuse for a party!

Spag bog night!

A spag bog night is a night to see how we deal with eating spaghetti (napkins at the ready!) washed down with Beaujolais, and followed by your cheesecake, before settling down to watch an eighties film. E.T. and Star Wars: Episode V – The Empire Strikes Back were popular American films of the eighties, but good British films included Chariots of Fire, Gandhi, The Missionary, Educating Rita, My Beautiful Laundrette, Withnail and I and A Passage to India.

Week 19 May 7–13

Theme

Remedies and home-made cures

The date 8 May is World Red Cross and Red Crescent Day, so this week we explore home remedies and foods to help recovery. The date 8 May 1945 was also Victory in Europe Day, or VE Day, when the allies accepted Germany's surrender in the Second World War. The street party atmosphere of VE Day gives us our excuse for a party this week. In honour of Red Cross and Red Crescent Day, hold a discussion about old cures for coughs and colds and have some sample cough sweets to try. Most people will have memories to share of family or local traditions in relation to remedies for common ailments and food and drinks that were given to help recovery. Discuss common medicines such as Milk of Magnesia, cod liver oil and Vicks VapoRub rubbed onto the chest! In Lincolnshire, folklore has it that rubbing warts with broad bean pods will get rid of the warts, and remedies for whooping cough include the more questionable practices of letting a horse breathe down the child's throat or eating a fried mouse! Elsewhere, sleeping on stones will cure your baldness and tying a dead mole around your neck will cure your toothache! There are many others, not all so bizarre, and some will have credibility – such as the practice of wearing a copper bracelet to relieve arthritic pain. Rosehip syrup was a common cure-all but it was not until the Second World War that its potential as a source of vitamin C was established – the Ministry of Food gave quite complicated instructions on how to make the syrup. You can still buy rosehip syrup, so have a bottle ready to give everyone a taste. Other foods given readily to help recovery are vitamin-rich fruit cordials, plenty of greens and good, honest, home-made broth or soup. Food brands such as Bovril, Marmite and Horlicks were seen as healthy additions to the diet, especially during the war years.

Food and mood

It is often said that food affects our mental health as well as our physical well-being. Debate this suggestion and discuss how food can improve your mood.

Check out the following links for information:

- www.bda.uk.com/foodfacts/FoodMood.pdf

- www.mind.org.uk/help/medical_and_alternative_care/food_and mood-the_mind_guide

Dandelion wine

The dandelion, a common 'weed', is said to have very good medicinal properties and is abundant at this time of year, often forming wonderful yellow carpets by the roadside but also being the scourge of many gardeners. So here is an easy recipe to make your own.

Take about 300 g dandelion petals (try not to get any green bits), steep them in a gallon of boiling water and leave this for 2 days. Strain the juice and add to it 2½ lb white sugar and the juice and zest from two oranges and two lemons. Boil the liquid until the sugar has dissolved, allow it to cool and then add ¾ oz winemaking yeast. Leave this fermenting for 3 days and then strain it into a glass demijohn with a bubble trap and let it ferment for a couple of months. After this, transfer it to another demijohn, allow the liquid to clear and then bottle it. The wine should be dry, crisp and light, with a wonderful aroma of summer.

Home brew and pickles

Ask your clients what home brew and pickles they made for themselves (eg beer, pickles, wines and jams) and if they enjoyed this, try making the same things again.

Activity
Food advertisements

Gather together a selection of large advertisements of various food products from magazines or newspapers. Stick these onto card and cover up the product name. If working in two teams, show both teams the advertisements and ask them to write down the product or brand name. Complete the quiz and then ask each team for their answers. Reveal the name of the product at the end. Try this with packaging from groceries such as cereal boxes, coffee jars, cake boxes and soup tins. This is more work and it might take a few weeks to collect the items, but it is more tactile, as the items can be handed around the group. A variation is to ask the price of the item and turn this into a two-part quiz: identify the brand and guess the price.

This week's excuse for a party!

Street party

Hold an indoor street party like those held outside on VE Day. This means having a long communal table down the middle of the room with everyone sat together. Let the group decide a theme for the party and decorate the room and table accordingly. Your dandelion wine will not be ready for a while, but it might be good to have a summer fete theme to welcome the better weather and shake off the winter blues. There must, of course, be summer music, dancing and good, old-fashioned party games. This gives you the opportunity to have a discussion about party games people played as both youngsters and adults. Try old favourites such as passing an orange along a line of people using only chins to hold the orange, or threading a spoon along the line through clothing! A popular party dance of old in Lincolnshire was the 'hokey-cokey' and a popular party team game was having a master of ceremonies asking teams to bring him or her such oddities as a bus ticket, a gentleman's sock or a comb.

Speechmark

Week 20

May 14–20

Theme

Fast food

On 18 May back in 1955 the first 'Wimpy' fast-food bar opened in London – it was in a small section of a Lyons teahouse, but it soon became popular and more Wimpy outlets opened, selling only hamburger meals. The concept came from the United States, inspired by the Popeye character 'Wimpy'. In the mid-1970s McDonald's arrived in the UK and became popular. Fast food has a long history, with ancient Roman street vendors selling bread and wine. Noodle shops were common in the East, as was the sale of falafel and flatbread in the Middle East. In mediaeval England most towns had 'cookhouses' that sold pies and market stalls selling cooked pasties. In 1762 the fourth Earl of Sandwich invented the sandwich, which is the staple of most packed lunches and office workers' breaks. Over the years there have been local variations, such as pie and mushy peas – in London, jellied eels were a cockney favourite. In coastal areas, seafood such as oysters and cockles are popular and it was the development of trawler fishing that brought about the British love affair with fish and chips. These days, however, the bulk of the fast foods consumed are burgers, fried chicken, kebabs and pizzas, with Indian and Chinese being popular as takeaways.

Fast-food memories

Ask the group to share their own experiences of takeaways and visiting fast-food cafés. Were these meals a special treat or part of the clients' regular diet? Also, explore what people had for their lunches at work. Did they take a packed lunch and, if so, what did it consist of?

What did they do if they had to prepare a quick meal at home – did they just make a sandwich or did they use up some leftovers?

A DIY burger

Here is a simple recipe for making your own burgers. Take 1½ lb minced beef, an egg, 1 tsp salt, ½ tsp black pepper, a cup of breadcrumbs, a quarter of a finely chopped red onion and 1 tbsp of Worcestershire sauce and thoroughly mix. Shape the mixture into burgers and cook them in a preheated frying pan with a little oil for 6 or so minutes on each side. Many burgers are served with lettuce, onion, sliced tomato, pickled gherkin, ketchup and mayonnaise. You can also add a processed cheese slice to convert it into a cheeseburger. Try making lots of mini burgers with tiny buns so that everybody gets to try one.

Activity

Super-size discussion

If you want to explore the issues of healthy eating, arrange to watch the documentary film *Super Size Me: A Film of Epic Portions* and discuss the trend for fast food. The world has moved a long way since Lyons' teahouses and now more than half of all meals eaten out are fast food. This is a worry for health experts, who tell us that the nation takes too little exercise and eats too much high-calorie fast food. Watch the film and ask your clients their thoughts about the debate.

Activity

(A)

Quick food quiz

What do we call deer meat?

Venison

What vegetable is the flower of a thistle?

Artichoke

What is couscous made from?

Wheat

What variety of beans are used in baked beans?

Haricot

What is a young pilchard called?

A sardine

The rice dish 'paella' comes from what country?

Spain

What country produces the most bananas?

India

Foods rich in starch such as bread and pasta are known as what?

Carbohydrates

What large fruit is called a beefsteak?

A tomato

What food grows without the need for sunlight?

Mushrooms

This week's excuse for a party!

Fast-food night out

Organise a group outing to a fast-food outlet such a burger restaurant. Try to encourage people to order a variety of different types of burger, and get the extras for all to try, such as fries, onion rings, and so forth. Also, get a variety of soft drinks for all to taste. After the meal have a discussion about the experience, quality and convenience of the food and whether people feel they could get used to eating these meals on a regular basis – if so, organise a regular trip or takeaway supper.

Week 21 May 21–27

Theme

Special diets, diabetes and recipes

There has been a recent and rapid increase in the number of people with diabetes in the UK, with up to 2.9 million people living with diabetes. Most of these people have type 2 diabetes and the rise is linked to increases in obesity. A significant proportion of these people are older adults, for whom the complications of diabetes can be harder to manage.

Special diets

Ask your clients to think about what other special diets they have come across and whether they have been subject to a strict food regimen at times. Discuss the difficulties of finding appropriate special foods and the cost of these compared with mainstream diets. Other diets to discuss are vegetarian, vegan, gluten-free, religious, Weight Watchers and sports diets. There are also many food intolerances such as lactose and egg. If you have several clients who have diabetes then seek out the services of a dietician who can help you ensure that these clients get varied and well-balanced diets suited to their individual needs and tastes.

Diabetes and recipes

Diabetes is a condition where the amount of sugar in the blood is difficult to control. Insulin normally does this for us but where no insulin is produced, as in type 1 diabetes, people will need to inject their own insulin. Type 2 diabetes is far more common; it is due to insufficient insulin and people have to manage their diet to stabilise their sugar levels. This is where special diabetic foods can be an enormous help. Especially valuable to diabetics are carbohydrates that are high in fibre such as wholemeal bread and pasta, vegetables, pulses and fruit, because these foods give us slow-release sugar. It is important to avoid a sudden rush of sugar, in the form of sweets, cakes, and so forth. This is where the following recipes can help, as they provide a tasty treat while avoiding too much sugar.

Chocolate and raisin biscuits (approximately 100 calories per biscuit)

Melt 5 oz low-fat margarine and 2½ oz soft brown sugar and mix in an egg, 2 tbsp water and 1 tsp vanilla essence. Mix together 2½ oz wholemeal flour and ½ tsp bicarbonate of soda and add 2 oz raisins, 1½ oz chocolate chips and 6 oz rolled oats. Add the liquid mixture to this, stirring well. Spoon small lumps onto a baking tray and flatten and cook for 12 minutes or so at 350°F until golden brown.

Carrot cake (approximately 150 calories per slice)

Beat four eggs and add 1½ cups vegetable cooking oil. In another bowl, mix together 2 tsp bicarbonate of soda, 1 tsp salt and 2 cups flour. Add this to the wet mixture, along with 2 tbsp vanilla essence and ½ cup apple juice. Stir into this 3 cups finely grated carrots, 1 cup sultanas and ½ cup chopped nuts. Pour this mixture into a baking tin and sprinkle more chopped nuts over the top. Bake the cake for 40 minutes at 325°F.

Activity

Food and cookery grid quiz

This is a quiz and game combined. This activity draws upon knowledge about food and cooking, and it is also easy to adapt to suit all abilities. Draw a bingo card on a flip chart or blackboard, five squares by five squares. Block out one square from each line and number the other squares from 1 to 20. You now have a numbered grid with four squares across and four squares down. Divide the group into teams and give alternate questions to each team, having tossed a coin to decide which team goes first. There are several ways of doing this. You can have counters or balls numbered 1 to 20 in a bag, which you pick out at random, and then that team wins that square if they get the question right. If they fail the ball goes back into the bag or you can offer it to the opposing side as a bonus, so that if you get it wrong your opponents could gain an advantage. Alternatively the teams can nominate which square they are going to play for. Vary the questions to include pictures. You then play as for bingo, in that the teams are trying to get a line up or down or all four corners. You can play it with both teams using the same grid (which is harder, because you are competing against your opponents for the squares) or using different grids. Use the quiz questions from elsewhere in this book or from other quiz books that you may have.

This week's excuse for a party!

Low-sugar party

This low-sugar party provides you with a good excuse for a trip to the local supermarket with your clients. The aim is to find low-sugar, diabetic-friendly items for a tea party and to enjoy it! Make sure you include a range of savoury and dessert items, and don't forget both soft and alcoholic drinks. Look for special diabetic biscuits and cakes and discuss their relative merits compared with non-diabetic foods.

Week 22 May 28–June 3

Theme

Italian food

The date 2 June is *Festa della Repubblica* or Republic Day in Italy. In 1946, following the fall of Fascism, Italians voted to be a republic rather than a monarchy. The Italian dish spaghetti bolognese was a huge favourite in the UK in the eighties and pizza is very popular in Britain, so this week's focus is Italian cuisine. Ask the group if anyone has been to Italy and sampled the fare.

Early Turkish settlers, Greek invaders and Saracens from North Africa influenced the food of Italy. Also, Italy is a huge country. Because of both these factors there are many regional foods, but the country is renowned for its pasta dishes and, of course, its pizzas, which originated in Naples. The Spanish are credited with introducing tomatoes into Italian cooking, which is of course a major ingredient in both pizza and pasta dishes. Olives are another essential ingredient, as are the cheeses mozzarella and ricotta. We had a spaghetti bolognese night in the eighties-themed Week 18, so we will concentrate on pizza this week. Ask the group for their experiences with pizza and ask about the different types they have tasted. Has anyone seen a pizza base being made and stretched in a restaurant or has anyone had a go at making a pizza base themselves? Here are two easy pizzas for the group to try.

Four-cheese pizza (pizza quattro formaggi)

Place 4 oz sliced mozzarella, 3 oz cubed goat's cheese, 4 oz cubed Dolcelatte cheese and 1 oz grated Parmesan into a bowl and mix. Spread some tomato pizza sauce over two medium-sized pizza bases and sprinkle the cheese over them with a little chopped oregano. Bake the pizzas at around 200°C.

Quick crumpet pizzas

Slice four tomatoes and grate 4 oz cheese. Grill the undersides of four crumpets. Turn them over and lay on the tomatoes and sprinkle with cheese and a tiny bit of oregano. Grill the crumpets slowly until the cheese melts. You can also do this with bagels and you can try adding mashed sardine or pepperoni.

Activity　Ⓐ

Food proverbs

Proverbs can be the basis of a simple quiz, with the group providing the ending to a proverb that you have begun – for example, Too many cooks …? Perhaps the best use, however, is to discuss the meaning of each proverb and explore the various interpretations. For example, what is meant by 'Still waters run deep'? Many proverbs also appear to contradict each other – for example, 'Too many cooks spoil the broth' but 'Many hands make light work'. The group can discuss these contradictions and ponder the circumstances in which each proverb might apply, as well as whether they are true or not. Here are some food-related proverbs.

- Forbidden fruit tastes sweetest.

- You can take a horse to water, but you can't make it drink.

- You can't teach your grandmother to suck eggs.

- Hunger is the best sauce.

- One rotten apple can spoil the barrel.

- Half a loaf is better than no bread.

- A watched pot never boils.

- It's no use crying over spilt milk.

- Enough is as good as a feast.

- Don't put all your eggs in one basket.

- Fine words butter no parsnips.

- One man's meat is another man's poison.

This week's excuse for a party!

Pizza takeaway night!

Decorate the room with all things Italian for this pizza takeaway night. Ask your travel agent for some posters and make an Italian collage from travel brochures. Buy a range of pizzas, each with a different topping, and slice them up so that everyone gets a taste of the different kinds. Supplement this with Italian wines such as Chianti and Pinot Grigio. The vodka-like grappa is a speciality that some might like to try, and fresh orange juice or lemonade are Italian non-alcoholic favourites. To enhance the Italian theme, play some Italian classical music such as opera, for which Italy is famous. Examples are Rossini's The Barber of Seville, Verdi's Rigoletto, La Traviata, Aida or Nabucco, and Puccini's Madame Butterfly. Other famous pieces are Vivaldi's The Four Seasons and Tomaso Albinoni's Adagio in G minor. There is also that famous song from 1962, 'Quando, Quando, Quando'!

Quick post-pizza Italian quiz

What is the large island just off the 'toe' of Italy called?
Sicily

Who painted The Last Supper?
Leonardo da Vinci

What town was buried when Mt Vesuvius erupted?
Pompeii

What emperor was murdered on the Ides of March?
Julius Caesar

What is the capital of Italy?
Rome

What is the topping on a pizza margherita?
  Tomato, basil and mozzarella

What is a flat biscuit filled with currants and named after an Italian leader?
  Garibaldi

Italy is shaped like what?
  A boot

What colours are on the Italian flag?
  Green, white and red

Which famous Italian city is built on islands?
  Venice

What mountain range stretches down the centre of Italy?
  The Apennines

Which Italian city has a leaning tower?
  Pisa

What is the largest lake in Italy?
  Lake Garda

Where are the headquarters of the Catholic Church?
  The Vatican

The Italian patron saint of animals is St Francis of …?
  Assisi

You can now relax with the second half of the Italian evening by watching an Italian-themed film. Three very good films to try are *Tea with Mussolini, Roman Holiday* or *La Dolce Vita*. More modern films include *The Italian Job* and the *Godfather* trilogy. Midway through the film you must have an interval at which is served the Italian invention of gelato, or ice cream. If the evening is a success, organise a visit to a local Italian restaurant.

Week 23 June 4–10

Theme

Portugal, biscuits and bars!

The date 10 June is Portugal National Day, but there is no connection with either biscuits or bars on this date, it is just an excuse for some varied activity. Portugal National Day commemorates the death in 1580 of Luís Vaz de Camões, who wrote an epic poem, *The Lusiads*, telling the story of Portugal's history and of famous explorers such as Vasco da Gama and Magellan. Ask your clients for their recollections of visiting Portugal on holiday. Portugal is famed for its fishing, as it has a large Atlantic coastline. It was the Portuguese explorer Vasco da Gama who discovered the sea route to the East and so brought back exotic spices and it was these seafarers who gave Portugal one of its staples, salted cod or bacalhau, which used to supplement the usual salted pork on long voyages – salt was used as a food preservative before the advent of refrigeration. Codfish, as it is known, is eaten as the Christmas dinner in some parts of Portugal and there are said to be 365 recipes for it, one for every day of the year.

Bacalhau

Soak 1 lb salted cod overnight. Boil the fish in water for 15 minutes, flake it and set it aside. Boil five large potatoes, slice and set aside. Slice two onions and a green pepper and crush two cloves of garlic and sauté these in olive oil. Place a layer of the potatoes in a casserole dish followed by a layer of the fish, then four sliced hard-boiled eggs, then the onion and pepper mix and sprinkle over this sliced black olives, some chopped parsley, the juice of a lemon and pour ½ cup olive oil over it. Bake the bacalhau at 350°F for 30 minutes.

Activity

Biscuits

Most of us have a sweet tooth and many people have a fondness for biscuits. Ask the group what their favourites are and take note of the responses – this will allow you to ensure these biscuits are kept in stock. Also ask about views on 'dunking' and if the group can remember buying biscuits loose. At many shops you could buy a selection of your own choosing, with the shop assistant picking the individual biscuits out of tins for you. When times were hard you could buy a bag of broken biscuits. Many people used to make their own biscuits too, so ask your clients for any old recipes they remember. Here are a few to try.

Ginger snaps

This is an old Be-Ro recipe. Mix together 8 oz flour, a pinch of salt, 1 tsp ground ginger and 4 oz caster sugar. In a pot, warm 3 oz margarine and 4 oz golden syrup and beat together. Add to this the dry mixture and one beaten egg, mixing thoroughly. Drop small dollops of the mixture onto a greased baking tray and bake the ginger snaps at 350°F for 15 minutes.

Oaties

Mix thoroughly 5 oz flour, 5 oz oatmeal, a pinch of salt and 3 oz sugar. Rub in 3 oz margarine and 3 tbsp milk to make a stiff paste. Roll the mixture out on a floured board and cut it with pastry cutters. Bake the oaties at 350°F for 15 minutes.

Chocolate biscuits

Mix 8 oz flour, 4 oz caster sugar and 3 tsp cocoa powder in a bowl and then rub in 4 oz margarine. Mix to a stiff paste with 3 tbsp milk and add 10 drops of vanilla essence. Roll out the mixture, cut it into biscuits and bake them for 15 minutes at 350°F.

Date biscuits

Follow the recipe for chocolate biscuits but substitute 4 oz chopped dates for the chocolate.

Almond biscuits

Take ¼ lb chopped almonds and add ¼ lb caster sugar and the grated peel of one lemon. Beat three egg yolks and add them to the mixture, and then add the well-beaten egg whites. This is an old recipe and merely tells you to bake 'crisply'!

Try experimenting with different icings and toppings too.

Activity

Beer-making kits

If your clients like a drop of beer occasionally, it is a good idea to get a kit to make your own beer. The equipment is inexpensive and it makes an excellent small group project.

JUNE

This week's excuse for a party!

The bar night

The idea for the bar night is that clients can look forward to a night out while not going anywhere! You re-create a bar in a room for the evening. Advertise the night in advance as a 'bar night' to make it special and to get people looking forward to it. You will need to rearrange the furniture to mimic a bar, with tables and chairs in small groups. Make the bar itself out of a table and have it well stocked with a range of drinks. You can canvas the clients beforehand for which drinks they will want. You will need some people to act as bar staff and waiters. Play traditional bar games such as cards, dominoes and darts. Serve plenty of bar-type snacks such as crisps. You might even have a piano player in a corner or some other sort of music event or dancing. The idea is for staff and clients to mix informally and to enjoy each other's company. Invite visitors and family to join you in order to make it even more sociable. Because of this week's Portuguese theme, don't forget the port and lemon!

Week 24 June 11–17

Theme

Picnics, barbecues and ice cream

Midsummer is a good time to think about alfresco events such as picnics, barbecues and summer delights such as ice cream.

Picnics

Ask your clients for their recollections of having picnics. Find out what their favourite picnic treats were, where their favourite picnic spots were and what they consider to be the essential ingredients for a picnic. The basis of most picnics is the humble sandwich, so ask the group what their favourite sandwich fillings are. Tastes vary, from the fondly remembered bread and dripping to schoolboy favourites such as ketchup or crisp sandwiches. Over the years we have become more adventurous with sandwiches, branching out from the simple cheese and pickle to embrace more exotic fillings such as Brie and grape. What is the weirdest sandwich people have tried?

Barbecues

Barbecues make great events in summer and they make a change from the usual evening meal. They are a good excuse for a group meeting to discuss the essentials and draw up a shopping list and organise the night. Visit the supermarket to buy a range of different burgers and barbecue items to try out. There may be some experts in the group and also those who can share their barbecue disasters! Try cooking the DIY burger from Week 20 on the 'barbie'! Barbecues also make good fundraising events.

Ice cream

Discuss the range of ice cream flavours and people's favourite ice creams. Ask the group if they can recall the ice cream vans and music they played and the variety of ice 'lollies' on offer alongside other delights such as choc ices. There were also many exotic ice cream concoctions that could be had at coffee bars and restaurants, such as the famous Knickerbocker Glory. Can the group remember all those extras that were so special, such as the chocolate Flake, hundreds and thousands, and chocolate and raspberry sauce?

Activity

Ice cream

To back up your reminiscence, take a group trip to the supermarket to buy a variety of flavoured ice creams, making sure you get everybody's favourite. Clients may be surprised to see how the humble ice cream has developed over the years into all sorts of frozen desserts such as Arctic rolls and fancy frozen cakes. Try a selection of sorbets too, and then try to make some of the following home-made ice creams to compare them with.

Quick ice cream

This is a very old wartime recipe. Take a small tin of evaporated milk and whip it up until it is stiff. Mix in 3 dessert spoons sugar and put it in the freezer for a few hours.

Vanilla and chocolate-chip ice cream

Beat two egg whites until stiff and then beat in 2 oz caster sugar bit by bit. In another bowl, beat 10 fl oz double cream until 'floppy'! In another bowl, mix two egg yolks with 2 tsp vanilla extract. Fold the cream mix into the egg white mix and then gradually fold in the yolk mix. Stir some grated milk chocolate into this, spoon it into a freezer tub and freeze for around 6 hours.

Honey ice cream

Boil 2 pints milk. Mix 2 oz cornflour into a paste with 2 tbsp milk and add this to the rest of the milk. Add 10 oz honey to the milk until it dissolves and then remove the pot from the heat. Allow the mixture to cool and then mix in 1 pint cream and freeze.

Activity
Birthdays

Birthdays are a great opportunity for food activity. While it is important that clients celebrate birthdays in their own way, staff will often wish to mark each client's birthday with some kind of celebration. If a party is being planned then there exists the opportunity for everybody to be involved to some degree in its preparation: buying presents, baking cakes, organising the games and music, setting the tables and organising the food and drinks. So, after discussing it with the person concerned, use these opportunities for activity.

Activity
Summer feast fundraiser

Summer is always a good time to hold fundraising events, as you can have stalls and seating outside. Besides the usual fundraising games and stalls you can buy some strawberries and cream to sell and call the event a Strawberry Fayre. Using this as a focus can give you many weeks' worth of activity beforehand making craftwork and baking cakes and biscuits to sell on the day.

This week's excuse for a party!

Picnic party

What people like about picnics and buffets are the variety of foods on offer and that they are usually small samples or finger foods so that you can try many things out. Discuss the range of possible foods with your clients and draw up a shopping and baking list of savoury and sweet items and drinks. Don't forget the cucumber and carrots to make into sticks, or the dips to go with them. The preparation for this can involve a sandwich-making production line, focusing on the clients' favourite fillings. Make the sandwiches special by cutting the crusts off and quartering the sandwiches diagonally. If the weather is fine have an alfresco buffet tea party and take some chairs outside and have a central buffet table or use your garden furniture. Some people may be happy to sit on rugs on the grass. This would be a good occasion to play some lawn games such as quoits or bowls, before finishing off with a selection of the group's favourite ice cream flavours served in traditional cones.

Week 25 June 18–24

Theme

Summer fruits

The date 24 June is traditionally Midsummer's Day in the UK, so this week we continue with our summer theme but with a particular food emphasis upon fruit. There are a large variety of fruits available today, so start this discussion by asking your clients to name as many fruits as they can and write these down on a flip chart. Ask them what fruit they had as children. Did they get fruit as a treat at Christmas and did they take an apple to school? Did they perhaps go 'scrumping' for apples and have they ever tried fruit picking? This might lead onto a discussion of other types of work in the fields, such as hop and potato picking. Ask clients what their favourite fruit is and what the most exotic fruit they have tried is. Ask them to name as many fruit-based drinks as they can, such as Ribena, lemonade, cider and orange juice. Have they ever made their own fruit drinks? Ask what their favourite fruit-based desserts are. Is it the humble apple pie, strawberries and cream or something more exotic such as a Knickerbocker Glory? Here are two old recipes for fruit trifles.

Banana trifle

Cut a Swiss roll into eight slices and arrange them in a trifle dish. Pour over them 1 cup warm milk and add a layer of sliced banana. Pour over this 1 pint custard and then gently place two more thinly sliced bananas on top. Carefully place dollops of whipped cream on top and grate some chocolate over it.

Sherry trifle

Slice a Swiss roll and arrange the slices in a trifle dish. Sprinkle the slices with 3 tbsp sherry. Pour the juice from a tin of pears over the slices and arrange the pears on top. Make a pint of strawberry jelly and, when cool, pour it over the slices and leave it to set. Make a pint of custard with 2 tbsp sherry added and, when cold, whisk it well and pour this over the jelly. Cover the trifle with whipped cream and decorate it with cherries or hundreds and thousands.

Activity

Fruit quiz

Which fruit contains the most calories?

Avocado

From what is Calvados spirit made?

Apples

What is a Chinese gooseberry?

A kiwi fruit

Which fruit has its seeds on the outside?

Strawberry

What is a cantaloupe?

A melon

The drink kirsch is flavoured with what?

Cherries

What do we call the rind of citrus fruits in cooking?

Zest

What fruit is commonly eaten in a salad?
Tomato

What are prunes?
Dried plums

What fruit is named after a port in Morocco?
Tangerine

What fruit is the French drink Grenadine made from?
The pomegranate

What percentage of a watermelon is water?
92 per cent

What harmful substance do apple pips contain?
Cyanide

What did sailors eat citrus fruit to prevent?
Scurvy

What fruit dessert is named after an opera singer?
Peach Melba

Activity

Seaside food trip

Any excuse for a trip to the seaside in summer is a good one. This trip is primarily to revisit the tastes of the seaside and the treats we loved as children. Such trips were often punctuated with candyfloss, bottles of pop, rock, toffee apples, and fish and chips. Make sure you visit a rock shop to recall the various fun items such as candy false teeth, dummies, and plates of rock breakfast! Then visit a seaside café for a typical 'sausage, egg and chips'-type dinner. Having filled up, take a stroll along the 'prom' to the arcades and 'lose' some money on the slot machines. One good idea is to give each person £1 in 2p pieces and see who has the most left after 30 minutes. Bingo should of course be indulged in. Then it will be time for another seaside cuppa before heading to the beach for a game of seaside bowls.

Seaside bowls

Mark out a crazy bowls course with 10 holes dug into the beach along the course. Mark each hole with a children's seaside flag. Players take it in turn to bowl around the course, rolling the ball along the sand.

Activity

Brambling

People will remember trips to the countryside for walks and many will recall picking brambles for their mother to make bramble pie or jam. Ask clients what other things they picked, such as mushrooms and flowers, and whether as children they collected conkers or acorns. Organise a trip to pick some brambles and then get the group to make a bramble pie.

Bramble and apple pie

Simmer some peeled and diced apples with some brambles, sugar and a little water for 15 minutes. Place a pie funnel in a pie dish and add the fruit. Sprinkle some brown sugar and lemon zest over this and then add the pastry crust. Put a hole in the centre and brush the top with milk. Bake the pie at 450°F for 30 minutes.

Activity
Smoothie maker

It is easy to make your own smoothies with a blender and this is an excellent way of getting a daily dose of vitamins and fruit. There are many variations you can try, such as banana and chocolate. Take ½ pint milk, 2 tbsp drinking chocolate powder, a banana and some ice cubes and blend. Try other combinations with the milk and ice such as strawberry and banana, or honey and yoghurt, and then just experiment with various fruit combinations.

This week's excuse for a party!

Exotic fruit night

Make fruit-themed collages to decorate the room for your exotic fruit night and then have prepared an exotic fruit tray. The idea here is to take a trip to the market or supermarket beforehand to buy samples of as many different types of fruit as you can. These are then prepared ready to eat and cut into small pieces and placed in bowls that can be passed around for all to take a piece of fruit to try. Ask clients to guess what the fruit is and where they think it comes from. Next, discuss the flavours and whether the clients like it or not. Indulge in your trifles and wash it all down with a special fruit punch, with or without alcohol, according to taste. Then settle down to watch a film with a summer theme such as *Summer Holiday* or *Mamma Mia!*

Week 26

June 25–July 1

Theme

Canadian food

Canada Day is celebrated on 1 July, commemorating the entry into force of the Constitution Act, 1867, which united three British colonies into one country. Being the second-largest country in the world, Canada has a wide range of foods. As usual, gather recollections of those who have travelled to or lived in Canada. Canada has a huge coastline and much of the north lies within the Arctic Circle. This being so, it has a long tradition of hunting and fishing. Further south on the plains, buffalo were hunted almost to extinction. These days the Canadians enjoy a much broader taste in food, heavily influenced by the French who colonised large parts of Canada. If there is a claim to the national dish it is probably poutine – French fries covered with cheese curds and gravy. Poutine is commonly sold as a fast food and it is as popular as burgers. Another national favourite is butter tarts, so try the recipe given here.

Butter tarts

Roll out 12 oz shortcrust pastry and use it to line small tart or muffin tins. Put 6 oz raisins, 4 oz butter, 6 oz brown sugar, 8 fl oz golden syrup and a pinch of salt into a pot and gently simmer the mixture until the sugar dissolves. Take the pot from the heat and stir in two beaten eggs and a teaspoon of vanilla extract. Pour the mixture into the tart shells. Bake the tarts for about 12 minutes at 425°F and then lower the heat and bake for another couple of minutes.

Maple syrup

Maple syrup was an indigenous food of the American Indians and it is still a favourite today, being used in many recipes in Canada. Maple syrup is made from the sap of maple trees, which is naturally sweet, boiled to form the syrup. Favourite ways to eat it are:

- spread on pancakes or waffles with butter
- as a maple blondie – take a chocolate brownie, top it with a scoop of vanilla ice cream, drizzle maple syrup over it and sprinkle chopped walnuts over it (NB: this one comes with a health warning!)
- instead of sugar in coffee!

Maple syrup cookies

Melt 180 g butter with 200 g caster sugar and allow to cool. Then mix in a large egg, 240 g plain flour, 60 mL maple syrup, 1 tsp vanilla extract, a pinch of salt and 2 tsp baking powder. Place the mixture in the fridge for an hour. Form the dough into balls and roll in caster sugar and flatten out. Bake the cookies on a tray at 180°C for around 10 minutes until they are brown.

Activity

Colloquialisms

Discuss the meaning of the following common expressions.

- Make no bones about it
- Fine kettle of fish
- Bring home the bacon

- A piece of cake
- The big cheese
- Selling like hot cakes
- Cherry-picked
- A fish out of water
- Cool as a cucumber
- Something fishy
- Couch potato
- Butter someone up
- Apple of my eye
- Walking on eggshells

Activity

Food bingo

The idea here is to replace numbers with pictures of food. So you will need to collect 20 different pictures of food products. Use a colour photocopier to print as many copies as you need for bingo cards and make up the bingo cards with different combinations of pictures. The caller then picks the pictures out of a hat at random. By getting clients to place counters over the food pictures as they are called out, the cards can be reused. It is best to use a five-by-five grid for the cards, with one square blank on each line (ie you will need 20 different food types). Prizes can be awarded for lines both up and down, for a full house and for all four corners.

Activity

More food quotations

A crust eaten in peace is better than a banquet partaken in anxiety.

Aesop

What's the difference between a boyfriend and a husband? About 30 pounds!

Anon

If at first you don't succeed, order a takeaway!

Anon

I cook with wine, sometimes I even add it to the food.

WC Fields

'Tis an ill cook that cannot lick his own fingers!

William Shakespeare

All sorrows are less with bread.

Miguel de Cervantes Saavedra

He was a bold man that first ate an oyster.

Jonathan Swift

After a full belly all is poetry.

Frank McCourt

In the end they will lay their freedom at our feet and say to us, 'Make us your slaves, but feed us.'

Fyodor Dostoyevsky

There is no love sincerer than the love of food.

George Bernard Shaw

This week's excuse for a party!

Musical night

On 28 June in 1902 Richard Rogers was born in New York. He wrote over 900 songs and 43 Broadway musicals including, in partnership with Oscar Hammerstein, *The Sound of Music, Oklahoma!, South Pacific* and *The King and I.* Ask clients if they can recall who starred in these films and what the special songs were from them. A few of Rogers' favourites were 'Oh, What a Beautiful Mornin'', 'People Will Say We're in Love', 'Some Enchanted Evening' and 'Climb Ev'ry Mountain'. Before the night, take a vote on which musical your clients want to watch and bake some chocolate brownies, maple cookies and butter tarts to have with a cup of tea at the interval. Musical nights go down very well and are great social occasions for sharing with relatives and friends.

Week 27

July 2–8

Theme

The United States

The North American theme continues with a focus on the United States in honour of 4 July, American Independence Day. Independence Day celebrates the birth of the United States in 1776 with the signing of the Declaration of Independence. People celebrate with picnics, barbecues and fireworks. There's no real need for recipes this week, as the hotdogs for the party make themselves. Open the tin, boil the frankfurters, place in a roll and smother with ketchup, mustard and fried onions. In the UK this is a fairground, seaside and football match treat and the smell of the frying onions will bring back such memories. The United States is of course the home of the hamburger, which we explored in Week 20, and both this and the hot dog have a claim to be the national dish. The Americans also lay claim to apple pie, as in the saying, 'It's as American as apple pie'! However, apple pie is really an English dish. The US quiz will help you trigger more reminiscences about the United States, so treat each question as an excuse for a discussion.

Activity

US quiz

Who was the famous cartoonist responsible for Mickey Mouse and friends?

Walt Disney

What is the film-making centre called?
Hollywood

What is the fizzy brown drink that is the Real Thing?
Coca-Cola

What stands 93 m high, guards the entrance to New York Harbour and was a gift from the French?
The Statue of Liberty

What spectacular waterfalls span the United States and Canada border?
Niagara Falls

What is the capital of the United States?
Washington, DC

What is North America's highest mountain?
Mount McKinley (Alaska, 6194 m)

What is the name of the bridge crossing a strait near San Francisco Bay and is also California's most famous landmark?
Golden Gate Bridge

What are the wetlands of Florida, home to alligators, called?
The Everglades

The Colorado River carved out the world's biggest gorge, located in Arizona. What is it called?
The Grand Canyon

New York is home to 8.3 million people. What other name does it have?
The Big Apple

When was the Declaration of Independence signed?

1776

What were the two sides in the American Civil War?

The Confederates and the Unionists

Which president was assassinated after the defeat of the Confederates in the Civil War in 1865?

Abraham Lincoln

Who were the two main stars in *Gone with the Wind*?

Clark Gable and Vivien Leigh

Who was the first president of the United States?

George Washington

Who were the three lead members of the Rat Pack?

Frank Sinatra, Dean Martin and Sammy Davis Jr

Which campaigner for civil rights is famous for his 'I Have a Dream' speech?

Martin Luther King Jr

What sport do Americans play with a bat and in which you can make a home run?

Baseball

Which bird is the symbol of the United States?

The bald eagle

Activity

Farming and gardening

Ask the group whether anyone worked or lived on a farm and if they can recollect old farming practices before the advent of machinery such as ploughing with horses and getting the corn in before combine harvesters were invented. Has anyone ever shorn a sheep or milked a cow? Did anyone grow vegetables or fruit in an attempt to be self-sufficient? Did anyone enter prize vegetables into competitions and do the clients have any secret pest control tips? Ask the group to describe their efforts at growing their own food and making their own jams and pickles.

Gardening inclusion

Clients can be given their own small vegetable plot to tend. Try to enlist the services of a local amateur gardener to work alongside the clients and give advice. You could also try growing plants from seed in individual plant pots and then pot the plants out as they grow to put onto the patio. Try tomato plants and others that can be grown on the windowsill. You could try getting a small terrarium or propagator and growing seedlings in this, or you could make your own by placing the top of a transparent plastic drinks bottle over the top of your plant pot and placing the pot in the sun – plant two to three seeds and transplant them out as they grow. If the group really enjoy all this then think about getting a greenhouse.

This week's excuse for a party!

American night

Decorate the room in red, white and blue and get the group to make some themed bunting. Create some collages on US themes using magazines and travel brochures. Small cupcakes can be baked and iced in red, white and blue. Hot dogs are the main food for the party. While the frankfurter comes from Germany, the idea of eating a frankfurter in a roll is said to originate from the United States. Hot dogs are a very popular American snack, and remember to have on hand plenty of that most popular of American drinks, Coca-Cola, to wash them down. Hold your US quiz in teams. Then settle down to watch an American-themed movie, which should be voted for beforehand and during which you should serve popcorn, another American favourite. Deciding which film to watch is a good group activity in itself. Ask the group to recall their favourite American actors, actresses and films – classics include Shane, Vertigo, Singin' in the Rain, The Odd Couple, Some Like It Hot and of course Gone with the Wind. Also, ask people if they can remember the popular series of 'Road to ...' films starring Bing Crosby and Bob Hope.

Week 28

July 9–15

Theme

France

The date 14 July is celebrated as Bastille Day in France. The French know it as *Fête de la Fédération*, celebrating the storming of the Bastille fortress and prison in 1789. This marked the beginning of the French Revolution and paved the way for the First Republic, founded in 1792. As France is the UK's closest continental neighbour, many clients will have visited France and will have memories they can share. It is a good idea to collect some travel brochures and do a large collage representing France and all things French – this will act as a good vehicle for reminiscence. Being so close, France has had a large influence upon the UK and vice versa, although neither the French nor the English like to think so! Food is important to the French, and while there are certain aspects of French cookery that have not been adopted in the UK, such as frog legs and snails, British cuisine has certainly been affected. There is considerable debate as to which came first, chips or French fries! The national dish of France is difficult to isolate, it being such a large country, but one traditional dish called 'pot-au-feu' has similarities with our own rural traditional stews. It was kept cooking continuously all winter in a big pot over the fire, being topped up as needed with root vegetables, steak and spices. Another popular dish is 'cassoulet', which is a casserole of white haricot beans with meat such as pork, lamb and sausage or duck. Chicken cooked in red wine, or 'coq au vin', is another popular meal. Two classic French dishes described here are boeuf bourguignon and crêpes.

Boeuf bourguignon

Boeuf bourguignon is essentially beef cooked in red wine. This recipe will serve around four people. Place 2 lb braising beef in a large bowl with a chopped onion, a sliced carrot, a crushed clove of garlic, 3 tbsp olive oil, three crushed peppercorns and a bottle of red wine and leave it to marinate for 2 hours. Remove the meat and reserve the marinade. Fry the meat in hot oil until browned all over. Add a clove of finely chopped garlic, sprinkle the meat with flour and cook at a high temperature for about 5 minutes. Add the marinade, sufficient to cover the meat, along with salt, pepper and a sprinkling of mixed herbs. Cover and simmer for 1½ hours. Fry some mushrooms and onions, add to the meat and marinade, and simmer for another 30 minutes.

Crêpes

Originating from Brittany, crêpes are basically thin pancakes. To make a good crêpe, mix 4 oz flour, a large pinch of salt and 1 tsp caster sugar in a bowl, make a well in the middle, add ½ pint milk and an egg and beat well. Next, pour a little batter into a heated, lightly buttered frying pan, moving the pan so the batter covers the base. Cook until the underside of the crêpe is browned and then flip it over and cook the other side. Crêpes can be eaten either sweet or savoury.

Champagne

Ask if your clients have ever tasted champagne. If not, I can't think of a more decadent excuse for fundraising!

Activity

Snacks

Most of us get peckish in between meals and just poke around in the cupboard for something or raid the biscuit tin. We often feel like a drink at odd times and just get up and put the kettle on or go to the fridge to get a can of drink or a glass of milk. In residential care this freedom can be eroded with clients only getting a drink and snack at preordained times. There is no reason why our clients should not have a small supply of favourite snack foods, which they have free access to, in their own rooms. Similarly, we need to be big enough to take risks and allow the clients to raid the fridge for a drink whenever they like and to put the kettle on without having to ask for permission. Clients can be taken to the shops to replenish their supplies on a regular basis. There is no reason why they should not have their own kettle and drink supplies in their own rooms. It is important to be able to have access to your own personal supplies, such as crisps, sweets and favourite biscuits, and to be able to decide when you will have a drink and when you will eat. These are basic human rights issues that are often overlooked, using the excuse that it is not practical or safe!

This week's excuse for a party!

French night

Use your French collage to decorate the room alongside blue, white and red bunting. Have some Parisian accordion music playing in the background and try this French-language quiz.

Escargot	Snails
Petit déjeuner	Breakfast
Frites	Chips
Œuf	Egg
Salle à manger	Dining room
Pain	Bread
Sucre	Sugar
Citron	Lemon
Pomme	Apple
Haricot	Bean
Pomme de terre	Potato
Bifteck	Steak
Poisson	Fish
Poulet	Chicken
Rosbif	Roast beef
Saucisson	Dry sausage
Fromage	Cheese
Lait	Milk
Glace	Ice cream
Bonbons	Sweets

Then settle down to watch a French-themed film such as *Gigi*, *Jean de Florette*, *The Day of the Jackal*, *The Three Musketeers*, *To Catch a Thief*, *Les Misérables* or *Amélie*.

Week 29 July 16–22

Theme

Belgium and chocolate

The date 21 July is Belgium's national holiday, commemorating the day in 1831 when Leopold took the oath as the first king of Belgium. Belgium is famed for its beer and chocolate-making, hence the excuse for another chocolate indulgence. The national dish of Belgium is arguably *moules frites* which is basically a bowl of mussels in a broth with Belgian chips and mayonnaise! *Frites* served with mayonnaise in a paper cone is a common street food in Belgium, and these chips are often accompanied by a minced meat-type of hot dog called a frikandel, which originates in the Netherlands. Belgian chocolate is considered to be the finest in the world, and much of it is still handmade in small shops using traditional equipment and methods. Praline chocolates, made with nuts, are a particular speciality and are often made in the shape of shells and shrimps. Beer is the national drink, and Belgian beers are hailed as the world's best. Try organising a Belgian beer tasting. Give each person a small glass and then pour out small amounts of different beers for each to taste. Gather comments upon each beer and see if people can discern much difference between them. Beers are also widely used in Belgian cooking, so try the following recipe.

Belgian beef and beer stew

Chop 3 lb beef into cubes and sprinkle the cubes with a little salt and pepper. Brown the cubes of meat a few at a time in hot butter, making sure each side is well done, and then place in a bowl and set aside. Melt 2 tbsp butter in a casserole dish and add two large onions, cut into rings about ¼ inch thick and then chopped in half, and slowly brown them for up to 15 minutes. Add two slices of bread made into fine breadcrumbs and brown these for a couple of minutes. Then stir in 2 cups beef stock and ½ pint strong Belgian beer and add a large sprig of thyme and a couple of bay leaves. Add 2 cups button mushrooms, halved and browned in butter, and a large carrot, sliced. Next, add the beef and its juices, with some more salt and black pepper, and simmer. Then, cover the casserole dish, place it in the oven and cook at 300°F for about 2 hours. Take the casserole dish out of the oven, add 1 tbsp mustard and 1 tbsp brown sugar, and return it to the oven for 15 minutes. This is a fine stew and one that you will want to come back to in the winter.

Chocolate

Chocolate contains chemicals that can lift the mood and arouse the passions. The Aztecs were apparently very fond of chocolate, and the Aztec emperor Montezuma drank many cups of chocolate a day to increase his ardour. Thus, chocolate is forever linked with romance. Interestingly, it was not until 1875 that chocolate was made in a solid form. Ask clients to share what their favourite type of chocolate is and keep a note of this list for birthdays and Christmas.

Home-made chocolate truffles

Gently heat 150 mL double cream in a pan. Remove the pan from the heat and add 100g chopped dark chocolate and 100 g chopped milk chocolate, stirring all the while until the chocolate is melted. Pour the liquid into a bowl and place in the fridge to cool for a while. When the mixture is firm, roll spoonfuls into small balls. To cover them you can roll some in cocoa powder, some in chopped nuts and some in coconut. For other variations, try adding Grand Marnier and some orange zest after you have melted the chocolate and this will give you chocolate orange truffles. Of course, adding rum will give you rum truffles, which can be rolled in chocolate hundreds and thousands.

Activity

An A–Z food quiz

This is a fun but challenging quiz. Write the alphabet in a column down one side of a flip chart and then just go from A to Z, identifying a food beginning with each letter. If you get stuck don't cheat, just go back to it throughout the day. If you get too good at this quiz, narrow your choice of foods down to just fruit and vegetables.

Activity

Food smells

This is a perception game to test our sense of smell – another fun activity. You will need some small, watertight containers. Black plastic film canisters are ideal for this, as you can't see inside and so guess what is causing the smell from its appearance. You will need to put some holes in the tops of the containers so that the smell of the contents can escape. The containers are passed around the group, with each member giving a suggestion as to what the smell is. Suggested contents for the containers are pine, mustard, horseradish sauce, mint, herbs, onions, vinegar, curry, lemon juice, garlic, ginger, tobacco and cloves. To stop liquids spilling, just soak a cotton wool ball in the liquid and place this in the canister. It is also good fun to have one container with nothing in it, to try to catch the group out.

This activity is usually good fun, and the facilitator can prompt suggestions by asking questions such as, 'Would you polish your shoes with it or would you put it in a sandwich?' Finish the session by inviting each client to share what their favourite food smells are – for example, fresh apples or bacon cooking.

This week's excuse for a party!

Another chocolate indulgence

Have a selection of different types of chocolate to taste, such as plain chocolate, milk chocolate, white chocolate, mint chocolate, chocolate with bubbles, rum-flavoured chocolate, chocolate with nuts and of course some Belgian chocolates. Hand the chocolates around for everyone to taste each sort, and gather people's opinions along the way. Have plenty of tea brewing to wash the ensuing thirst away. Follow this with a viewing of the film *Chocolat* and have an interval to serve chocolate ice cream and choc ices.

Week 30
July 23–29

Theme

The (not so) Roaring Twenties

The 1920s were a time of huge change in many aspects of life, especially politically and culturally. Hopes for a better future following the First World War were at odds with the high rates of unemployment and poverty, which culminated in the General Strike of 1926. Big political changes were occurring with the formation of the communist Union of Soviet Socialist Republics in 1922 and the rise of fascism in Germany and Italy. In the UK, democracy was increasing with everyone over the age of 21 getting the vote in 1928, and high unemployment helped the rise of the Labour Party. This period also saw significant changes in popular culture with the rise of jazz music and the bright angular designs of the art deco period. The Charleston was the popular dance and 'cocktails' were the new drinks craze. Fashions were changing too, with a move towards shorter dresses and short hair for women. On the home front, Bakelite was appearing everywhere. This versatile dark-brown material was especially useful for electrical equipment such as plugs. British toy manufacturers were also entering a new era, with Meccano producing popular building sets as well as Hornby model railways and Dinky cars. On the food front, cakes were popular and with ingredients becoming available again after the war, home baking had a resurgence. The era became known as the cake era, and afternoon tea at Lyons' Corner Houses was very popular in London.

Angel cake

This cake was very popular and was called angel cake because it uses only the whites of eggs, the yolks being saved for making pasta and noodles. Whisk six egg whites, 1 tsp cream of tartar and 1 tsp vanilla extract until the mixture stiffens. Whisk in 1½ cups sugar and a pinch of salt, and then fold in 1 cup plain flour. Pour the mixture into a baking tin and bake for 40 minutes at 350°F. When cool it can be cut in half, the middle spread with jam and the top sprinkled with icing sugar.

There are many variations on such sponges, with poorer households using even simpler recipes. This recipe from *Foulsham's Universal Cookery Book* gives the following no-nonsense instructions:

> 1 pound flour, 1¼ pound sugar, 5 eggs, rind of 1 lemon, a 'little' brandy. Mix dry ingredients, beat in eggs, yolks and whites mixed separately. Add brandy, beat very thoroughly. Bake in quick oven.

Discussion activity

Some notable events of the 1920s

1920   The National Football League is formed; Prohibition begins in the United States; rioting in Belfast; women admitted to Oxford University; Rupert Bear first appears in the Daily Express.

1921   Mussolini becomes 'Il Duce', the leader of the National Fascist Party in Italy; free school milk is introduced to combat tooth decay and calcium deficiencies; Einstein wins the Nobel

Prize in Physics; the province of Northern Ireland is created;
the British Legion holds its first Legion Poppy Day.

1922   The British Broadcasting Corporation is formed, as is
Birdseye Seafoods Inc; James Joyce's *Ulysses* is published;
archaeologist Howard Carter finds the entrance to
Tutankhamen's tomb.

1923   Wembley Stadium opens to the public and holds the first FA
Cup Final, played between Bolton Wanderers and West Ham
United; exuberant crowds way in excess of the stadium's
125,000 capacity are cleared from the pitch by police on
horseback; Bolton Wanderers win 2–0; Prince Albert, Duke
of York, weds Lady Elizabeth Bowes-Lyon.

1924   The Labour Party come to power for the first time, with
Ramsey MacDonald as prime minister; in Russia, Vladimir
Ilich Lenin dies and is replaced by Joseph Stalin; the first
refrigerators are marketed in the UK.

1925   A Rolls-Royce costs just £1,900 and Britons are encouraged
to immigrate to Australia; construction begins on the first
Mersey road tunnel, the Queensway Tunnel.

1926   John Logie Baird demonstrates the television; AA Milne's
Winnie-the-Pooh is published; the General Strike begins;
Agatha Christie disappears; red telephone boxes appear for
the first time.

1927   A hard, freezing winter of blizzards; the first 'talkie', *The Jazz
Singer*, is released; the first transatlantic telephone call is
made from London to New York; Joe Davis wins his first
World Snooker Championship.

1928   Women are allowed to compete in athletics and gymnastics at the Olympics for the first time; 'Dixie' Dean scores 60 goals in a season as Everton win the football league; the first outing for the Flying Scotsman; Alexander Fleming discovers penicillin; the Tyne Bridge opens, connecting Newcastle upon Tyne with Gateshead.

1929   The airmail service begins and the first traffic lights are used in London; the Wall Street stock market crashes; the first Tesco store opens in Burnt Oak, Edgware, Middlesex.

Activity

Radio night

John Logie Baird was still perfecting the television in the 1920s and for most people it was a case of sitting by the radio for quite a few years yet. Ask your clients if they think that many people today would find it difficult to just sit and listen. Try it for yourselves. Look through the radio listings as a group and choose a programme to listen to together. Agatha Christie was very popular in the twenties too, so get an audiobook version of a popular Poirot story and sit around 'the wireless' and listen together. Don't forget the half-time tea and cake!

Activity

Home-made ice lollies

With the twenties seeing the first refrigerators being sold in the UK, and while it is still summer, making your own ice lollies is a good idea. Ask your clients what their favourite flavours were from childhood, and then discuss the possibilities by asking them to dream up new flavours. Ice lollies are easy to make using moulds and small sticks. Try pure fruit juice, smoothies, fizzy drinks, 'instant' dessert mixes and undiluted blackcurrant cordial. Try two-layer lollies with instant dessert mixes and try adding chocolate drops or small pieces of fruit.

This week's excuse for a party!

Twenties night

Hold a twenties quiz based on the information outlined for this week and serve tea and cakes. Then settle down to watch *The Great Gatsby*. This novel by F Scott Fitzgerald is set in 1922, at the height of the Roaring Twenties. Alternatively, watch any of the Agatha Christie Poirot films set in this era. Round the night off with a crème de menthe, Poirot's favourite spirit.

Week 31   July 30–August 5

Theme

Meat

The diets of many cultures centre on meat dishes and the focus this week looks in particular at some less-expensive meat-based foods. When British meat stocks were running low during the Second World War, the United States agreed to send much-needed supplies, and these included Spam.

Spam

Spam, or 'spiced ham', is one of those love-it-or-hate-it foods. Sometimes called 'poor man's meat', Spam was a staple of the 1940s. It is basically chopped pork and ham sold in a tin and with salt and preservatives to give it a long shelf life. Spam was popular in the UK during the war when meat rationing was in force. One essential and common Spam experience was fried Spam – slices of Spam fried in hot butter until browned on each side. This was often eaten at breakfast with eggs or for dinner with potatoes and vegetables. Spam was also a good ingredient to use to spice up leftovers – for example, cubed and fried Spam with last night's potato and cabbage leftovers, a sort of deluxe bubble and squeak! Another common use of Spam was in a sandwich, accompanied by liberal quantities of ketchup – luncheon meat, minced ham mixed with cereal, was another variety of Spam. However, the most famous use of Spam was in the legendary Spam fritter! This is a slice of Spam fried in batter. During the Second World War, Spam fritters were popular with chips and mushy peas instead of fish and chips, as fishing became dangerous.

Corned beef

Corned beef fritters were also a chip shop favourite because of the shortage of fish. Corned beef is salt-cured beef and it dates far back in history, long before the process of canning was invented. The canned variety of corned beef was of course another staple of the war years, when other meats were scarce. Much of the beef came from Uruguay and the company Fray Bentos. In the UK it is often called 'bully beef'. One of the best uses was in the popular 'corned beef hash'.

Corned beef hash

Corned beef hash is corned beef mashed up and cooked in a large pan together with whatever else is available, usually onions and potatoes, until it is crispy brown. This was often served as a breakfast food with eggs and fried leftover potatoes, and many ate it with baked beans. It could also be shaped into balls before being fried. Others added diced carrots and stock cubes. Two versions are outlined here.

For the first version, put four diced carrots, a large diced onion and three diced potatoes into a pot and just cover them with water. Boil the vegetables over a medium heat, adding salt and pepper to taste. Mix two stock cubes with a little water and add this to the pot. Add a tin of corned beef, cubed, some chopped mushrooms and a tin of tomatoes. Bring to the boil and then simmer until the vegetables are cooked.

For the second version, fry diced corned beef, mushrooms and sliced onions in a pan. When these are cooked, place them in a casserole dish and pour a tin of baked beans over them. Slice parboiled potatoes and place them on top of the beans. Pour a tin of tomato soup over the potatoes. Sprinkle grated cheese over the top and bake at 180°C for around 40 minutes.

Activity

Meat quiz

What does Spam mean?
> *Spiced ham*

What is bouillabaisse?
> *Fish soup*

What part of a cow is tripe?
> *The stomach lining*

What is a John Dory?
> *A fish*

What type of meat is generally used in moussaka?
> *Lamb*

Beef Wellington is a steak wrapped in what?
> *Puff pastry*

What meat is in cock-a-leekie soup?
> *Chicken*

How do you turn a herring into a kipper?
> *Smoke it*

What is sushi?

Raw fish or seafood with vinegared rice often wrapped in seaweed

What is traditionally used to make brawn?

A pig's head

What does 'corned' in corned beef refer to?

Salt

What type of sauce is usually served with pork?

Apple

What do we call meat prepared according to the Koran?

Halal

What is the traditional meat in a kebab?

Lamb

What is kedgeree?

A dish consisting mainly of boiled rice, cooked fish and hard-boiled eggs

What is the traditional casing of a haggis?

A sheep's stomach lining

The chorizo is associated with which country?

Spain

What is Bombay duck?

An Indian fish dish

What is a flitch?

A side of salted and cured bacon

What Italian city gives its name to a type of ham?

Parma

This week's excuse for a party!

Sausage night

The sausage is a favourite form of meat the world over and dates back more than 5,000 years. Sausages are basically ground-up meat covered in a casing of intestine, although many artificial casings are used these days. Many people will have their favourite sausage recipes, such as toad-in-the-hole, bangers and mash or sausage casserole. There are also regional variations such as the Cumberland and Lincolnshire sausage, each of which lays claim to the fiercely contested title of the best British sausage. The nickname 'bangers' derives from the fact that sausages can 'explode' as the water content expands during cooking. Take a trip to your local butcher or supermarket and buy a range of different types of sausage. Check out the local non-English food outlets too, as they can have some interesting varieties such as German frankfurters and eastern European salamis. Cook all of the sausages, chop them into bite-sized pieces, stick cocktail sticks in them and hold a tasting session, discussing which types people prefer. An alternative is to have a hot dog night, complete with fried onions, mustard and ketchup, while watching a food-themed film such as *Babette's Feast* or *Ratatouille* or holding a food quiz.

Week 32 August 6–12

Theme

Vegetarian food and carrots

Vegetarianism is becoming increasingly popular and is considered to be a healthy diet. Indeed, the bulk of what we eat is vegetable matter and in times of hardship it becomes our staple source of food. See Week 27 for discussion ideas relating to gardens and people's attempts at growing their own vegetables. Many of us will have made some attempts at growing the odd tomato in the greenhouse and others will have recipes for vegetarian meals to share from when they could not afford to eat meat. The war years were one such time, with parks and window boxes given over to vegetable growing. A favourite wartime recipe was the humble vegetable turnover.

Vegetable turnover

Sift 12 oz plain flour with 3 tsp baking powder and a pinch of salt and rub into it 3 oz of margarine or dripping. Bind the pastry with a bit of water and set aside. Dice four cooked carrots and six cooked potatoes and then mix them together with salt and pepper to taste. Mix in a finely chopped and lightly fried onion. Divide the pastry into four pieces and roll them out, adding the vegetable mix and forming into pasties. Press down the edges to close them, prick the tops with a fork, brush the tops with milk and bake at 220°C for 30 minutes.

Carrots

The carrot, in particular, became an important part of the British diet during the war years, as it was in plentiful supply thanks to the 'Dig for Victory' campaign. It was used as a substitute for other foodstuffs such as sugar and it proved very versatile, being high in fibre and a good source of nutrients such as vitamin A, which is good for vision, bones, teeth and skin. The Ministry of Food introduced a children's cartoon character called Doctor Carrot to promote carrots as a nutritious food source – Doctor Carrot was depicted skipping along carrying a bag of vitamin A. The ministry also issued many recipe leaflets and promoted the idea that carrots helped you see better in the blackout: 'A carrot a day keeps the blackout at bay'! These inventive recipes included carrot jam, curried carrot, carrot fudge and carrot croquettes.

Carrot fudge

Put 4 tbsp finely grated carrot in a pot, add just enough water to cover it and cook it for 10 minutes, adding some orange squash. Melt a gelatine leaf into the carrot and stir for another few minutes, and then pour into a flat dish and let it set.

Carrot croquettes

Boil six carrots until tender and then dry and mash them, adding salt and pepper to taste. Make a thick sauce with 1 oz margarine, 10 oz cornflour and ¼ pint milk. Add the mashed carrot and shape into croquettes. Roll the croquettes in oatmeal and fry them in hot fat.

Carrot and oatmeal casserole

Dice ½ lb carrots, ¼ lb potatoes and ¼ lb other root vegetables such as swede or turnips. Fry the vegetables in dripping and stir in 2 oz oatmeal until all the dripping is absorbed. Add salt, pepper and herbs according to taste. Add a meat extract cube and a pint of vegetable stock and simmer for an hour.

Activity

Vegetable guess and tasting

Arrange a series of dishes, each containing small pieces of vegetable either cooked or uncooked. Get some unusual varieties from your local delicatessen or supermarket. Then simply ask your clients to taste the dishes and guess what vegetables they are. Have whole examples of some of the more unusual vegetables for people to see and feel and guess what they are.

Activity

Meat substitutes

These days there are a range of meat substitutes on the market that are part of many vegetarian diets. Cook a range of these vegetarian burgers, substitute bacon slices, vegetarian sausages and chicken-type nuggets, provide some dips to accompany them and see what the clients think of them. Also, try making a chicken casserole with chicken-type chunks and have a full meal tasting.

This week's excuse for a party!

Carrot night!

With so many carrot-based recipes this week it has to be a carrot party. Have a meal using some carrot recipes and follow it with this vegetable quiz.

What is a shiitake?   A mushroom

Fried cabbage and potatoes is known as what?
   Bubble and squeak

If a dish is 'à la florentine', what is in it?   Spinach

What is a 'petit pois'?   A pea

What is a mangetout?   A pea with an edible pod

Which member of the onion family is said to protect you from vampires?
   Garlic

What vegetable is also called an 'eggplant'?
   Aubergine

If a dish is Parmentier, it is served with what?
   Potatoes

What is laver bread made from?   Seaweed

What are crudités?
   Sliced or shredded raw vegetables served as an hors d'oeuvre and often with a dip

What are hash browns made from?   Potatoes

A savoy is a variety of what?   Cabbage

What is the main ingredient of sauerkraut?
    Cabbage

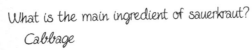
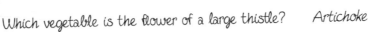

Which vegetable is the flower of a large thistle?   Artichoke

What do you call a dish made primarily from green peppers, aubergines and tomato sauce?
    Ratatouille

What variety of beans are used in baked beans?   Haricot

The American 'zucchini' is called what in the UK?   Courgette

The eastern European soup 'borscht' is made from what?
    Beetroot

Which steak is a fruit?   Beefsteak tomato

What are pommes de terre?   Potatoes

Following this, round the night off with *The Land Girls*, a good film to watch together and one that is in keeping with the 'Dig for Victory' theme. Have an interval and serve some carrot biscuits from this old wartime recipe.

Carrot biscuits

Cream 2 tbsp margarine and 4 tbsp sugar, and then beat in two drops of vanilla essence and 8 tbsp grated carrot. Fold in 12 tbsp flour and 1 tsp baking powder. Dollop spoonfuls of the mixture onto a baking tray and bake the biscuits at 180°C for around 20 minutes.

Week 33 August 13–19

Theme
Indian food

The date 15 August is India's Independence Day. On this day in 1947 India gained independence from British rule and became a sovereign nation. India is associated with spicy food, so begin with an exploration of the group's taste for hot and spicy foods. Ask if anyone has travelled to India and sampled the real thing. Then explore your clients' experiences of visiting Indian restaurants and cooking their own curries. There is much more to Indian food than curry. India is a large and ethnically diverse country and thus has many regional specialities and different ways of cooking. Flat breads such as chapattis are popular, as is seafood because of the long coastline. Rice is also a staple accompaniment, and the cuisine of India has a large range of vegetarian dishes. Indian dishes are so popular in the UK that the nation's favourite dish is often cited as chicken tikka masala! The growth in Indian takeaway restaurants has been phenomenal, showing that British tastes are by no means conservative. This is not a recent phenomenon, as the first UK Indian restaurant dates back to 1809. Key accompaniments to Indian curries are various samosas, bhajis and chapattis.

Onion bhaji

Bhajis are basically deep-fried 'fritters' and are quite easy to make. Beat two large eggs in a bowl. Stir into this two halved and thinly sliced medium onions and 1 oz chopped fresh coriander. Mix 4 oz gram flour, ¼ tsp chilli powder, ½ tsp turmeric, ½ tsp cumin powder, ½ tsp baking powder and a large pinch of salt in a bowl and add this to the wet mix, stirring well. Form the mixture into balls and fry these in hot vegetable oil for around 30 seconds on each side until browned.

Vegetable samosa

Samosas are triangular baked or fried pastries with savoury fillings. Take a large, diced, cooked potato, 1 oz defrosted frozen peas, half a diced and fried onion, 1 oz tinned sweetcorn, half a grated carrot and 1 tsp each of cumin, coriander and curry powder and mix it all together. Take 4-inch square sheets of filo pastry, drop a tablespoon of filling into the centre of each square and fold the square diagonally in half, thus forming a triangle. Brush the edges of the pastry with beaten egg and press them together. Fry the samosas in a deep-fryer at 350°F until golden.

Chapatti

For a simple chapatti, mix 6 oz chapatti flour with a large pinch of salt, make a well in the flour and then slowly add water, mixing until you get a smooth dough. Put some vegetable oil on your hands to stop it sticking and knead the dough until it is soft. Divide the dough into six pieces, shape the pieces into balls and then roll them out on a floured surface to about 6 inches in diameter. Heat the chapattis in a hot frying pan, turning them so they brown on both sides.

Activity

Spice quiz

This is a real treat for the nose and a real test of our sense of smell. Many spices are used in cooking but do we know what they are and can we recognise them? Arrange a wide selection of herbs and spices in saucers. These are then passed around for all to smell, identify and comment. This can be done in teams, with each saucer given a number and the teams going around writing down their guess for each saucer. Common spices and herbs to use include paprika, vanilla pods, curry powder, aniseed, basil, cinnamon, coriander, cumin, fennel, garlic, ginger, mustard, mint, lemon verbena, nutmeg, rosemary, sage, saffron, thyme and turmeric.

Activity

Food pillow guess

This activity is great fun and can be repeated regularly. The degree of difficulty can be varied to suit all groups, from very easy to very difficult. This exercise also helps with our powers of communication and description. Basically, you need a pillowcase and into this you put an object and tie up the top of the pillowcase. You then pass it around and the members of the group have to guess what is in the pillowcase by feeling it. Get each client to say what they think it is and get them to describe it in as much detail as possible – shape, size, weight, texture, and so forth. All of these factors supply clues as to the identity of the mystery object. Try cookery and baking instruments such as a handheld whisk, and move onto objects such as vegetables and fruits and other ingredients.

This week's excuse for a party!

Curry night

Decorate the room and the dining table with Indian themes, posters and collages you have made earlier in the week. Indian saris are highly coloured and you can make some colourful glittery bunting to add to the atmosphere. Order in mild curry and have some of your bhajis, samosas and chapattis that you prepared earlier. Play some authentic Indian music and then enjoy your meal. Have plenty of water and Indian lager on hand for people to quench their thirsts and cool their mouths if the food proves too spicy for them! It might be possible for a local school or Indian group to come along and entertain the group with some traditional dancing. They may even offer to cook for you next time!

To round the night off, watch one of the very good Indian-themed films such as *East is East*, *Monsoon Wedding* or *Bend it like Beckham*, or one of the more traditional film such as the classics *Gandhi* or *A Passage to India*.

If the clients enjoy these foods and themes then why not organise a trip to an Indian restaurant.

Week 34   August 20–26

Theme

Back to the 1930s

In the 1930s, Hitler was rising to power in Germany and there were troubles in China, India, the West Indies and the Middle East. In the UK, unemployment hit 3 million and many were still living in poverty, although many were also enjoying a rise in living standards, so it was a time of contrasting fortunes, of the 'haves' and the 'have-nots', of decadence for some and poverty for others amid cultural change and modernisation under the shadow of the oncoming war. Transport links increased and the classic British Rail and London Underground posters of that era evoke a time of pleasure, holidays and trips. Food-wise, a dozen eggs cost a shilling or 5p (today they cost around £2.50) and tinned foods such as beans and peaches were becoming increasingly common, as was frozen food. Sweets were also on the increase with such brands as Kit Kat, Smarties, Rolo and Mars bars, which would have cost you 2d each (just under 1p). Boxes of chocolates also came on the scene with the likes of Black Magic, Quality Street and Cadbury's Roses. The year 1930 saw sliced bread sold in the UK for the first time, and by the end of the 1930s instant coffee had migrated across from the United States too. The year 1937 saw the introduction of cheap tinned meat such as Spam (see Week 31). This was a far cry from the decadent life of the young and rich, who were more concerned with cocktail parties, Hollywood and dancing. Many of our current eating habits were emerging at this time, and there was an increase in magazines aimed at the housewife. One such magazine was *Woman and Home*, which was subtitled 'a magazine of delightful suggestions'. Such magazines were full of recipes and advice on cleaning and cooking. One popular recipe was marmalade pudding.

Marmalade pudding

Warm ¼ pint milk with 1 oz margarine and crumble five slices of bread into this. Add 2 tbsp flour, 1 tbsp sugar, 1 tbsp marmalade and a beaten egg. Mix well and add 1 tsp baking powder. Put 3 tbsp marmalade in a pudding basin, pour the mix on top and steam for 1½ hours.

Marmalade cake

Beat 4 oz sugar and 4 oz margarine to a paste in a warm basin. Mix in 4 oz marmalade and then gradually stir in 8 oz flour and two beaten eggs with 4 tbsp milk. Mix it well. Bake in a greased cake tin for around 1¼ hours at 350°F.

Discussion activity
Some notable events of the 1930s

1930 Frozen foods go on sale in the UK; Amy Johnson flies solo from England to Australia; the first football World Cup takes place in Uruguay and Uruguay beat Argentina 4–2 in the final – England does not play, as Uruguay is deemed too far to travel.

1931 Oswald Mosley and his 'Blackshirts' come on the scene; trolleybuses come to London; Gandhi, dressed in a loincloth, meets King George V and Queen Mary at Buckingham Palace; the Empire State Building opens in New York.

1932   Éamon de Valera becomes prime minister in Ireland and the first test match between India and England takes place at Lord's; hunger marchers from Glasgow reach London and Labour leader Ramsay MacDonald refuses to see them; *Woman's Own* published.

1933   Prohibition ends in the United States; Hitler becomes Chancellor of Germany; George Orwell's *Down and Out in Paris and London* is published; Fred Perry wins US tennis championship.

1934   The first Mersey road tunnel, the Queensway Tunnel, is opened in the UK; 266 are killed in the Gresford Disaster, an explosion in a Welsh colliery.

1935   King George V's Silver Jubilee is celebrated; Mao Tse-tung becomes the leader of communist China; driving test and L-plates are introduced in the UK.

1936   The Jarrow March occurs with 207 unemployed workers marching the 300 plus miles to London to protest against their unemployment and the poverty in the north; Edward VIII abdicates to free him to marry Wallis Simpson; the black athlete Jesse Owens wins the 200 m race at the Berlin Olympics and Hitler refuses to shake his hand; this year also gave us the game Monopoly!

AUGUST

1937   George VI is crowned; the airship Hindenburg catches fire, killing 33; civil war breaks out in Spain; *The Dandy* is first published and the film *Snow White and the Seven Dwarfs* is released.

1938   Neville Chamberlain returns from negotiations with Hitler and Mussolini in Germany to declare that there will be 'peace for our time'; the London Zoo opens; the Beano comic appears.

1939   War is declared in Europe; free air-raid shelters are delivered to London homes and the lights are blacked out; 1½ million children are evacuated from UK cities to the countryside; Germany and Russia invade Poland; the film *Gone with the Wind* is released.

This week's excuse for a party!

PARTY TIME

Thirties party

A Hollywood-style thirties party is an excuse to focus upon the decadence rather than the poverty of the thirties. Many people 'escaped' the Great Depression by going to the 'movies'. Stars of the era included Greta Garbo, Fred Astaire, James Cagney and the Marx Brothers, and it was the time of the Busby Berkeley Babes. The United States let its hair down with the end of Prohibition and the popularity of 'swing' bands. So decorate the room in thirties style and make collages of stars from thirties Hollywood movies. Use the colour scheme of black, white and silver to give the party a period feel and play big band swing music. Hold a thirties 'Name that Tune' quiz and encourage dancing. Prepare a buffet with sandwiches, olives, savouries, small cakes, and so forth, and then try a few cocktails before sitting down to watch a good Hollywood movie.

Week 35 — August 27–Sept 2

Theme

Drinks

On 31 August in 1900 Coca-Cola went on sale in the UK for the first time, so this week we focus on the wide range of drinks available. There are a huge range of fruit juices and soft drinks available these days. Many of us will have a favourite soft drink, such as cola, but can people remember the less common ones such as dandelion and burdock? Ask clients to recall the drinks from their childhood and if they can remember getting free milk at school. What drinks were they given when they were ill? Have they all tried Lucozade? Arrange for a tasting with old favourites such as Tizer, real lemonade, ginger beer and Dr Pepper. Also, try a range of modern fruit juices and smoothies – another good excuse for a shopping trip. You can also see if people can tell the difference between Coca-Cola and Pepsi! Go on to discuss what people's favourite nightcap is and be sure to make a note of this for future reference.

Drinks to try

- A glass of hot water with a teaspoon of honey and the juice of half a lemon

- Hot milk with honey

- Try cordials with hot water instead of cold

Also try the following recipes.

- Strawberry milkshake. Blend 12 oz strawberries with 1½ tbsp caster sugar. Force through a sieve to get rid of the seeds. Blend this again with a pint of skimmed milk and ½ pint of natural low-fat yoghurt. Try this with other fruits too.

- Tomato juice. Blend together 1 lb ripe tomatoes, 1 tsp salt, 1 tsp Worcestershire sauce, 1 tsp brown sugar, ½ pint water and the juice of half a lemon.

- Claret cup. Pour a pint of claret into a jug and add about 15 thin slices of cucumber and a sliced lemon. Stir in ½ lb caster sugar and ½ pint each of lemonade and soda water. Strain the drink and serve with ice.

- Shandy gaff. Take a pint of pale ale and a pint of ginger beer and pour it into a jug containing chopped ice filling the first 2 inches of the jug.

Activity

Drinks quiz

What drink is Worcestershire sauce traditionally added to?

Tomato juice

What is the oldest soft drink first sold in 1885?

Dr Pepper

If you were drinking a cordial of *Ribes nigrum* what would you be drinking?

Blackcurrant juice

What drink is often referred to as Adam's ale?

Water

What is the world's best-selling soft drink?

Coca-Cola

What was invented in Nazi Germany when Coca-Cola was no longer available?

Fanta

What popular glucose drink is given to the ill?

Lucozade

Which drink claimed to be a vigorous tonic?

Vimto

What drink is named after an upset stomach?

Pepsi (dyspepsia)

What drink is traditionally given to players at Wimbledon?

Barley water

Activity

Drinks word search

Find the following words hidden in the grid.

juice	Pepsi	coffee	Irn-Bru
cola	tea	claret	ale
milk	Tizer	port	Tango
beer	water	cocoa	cider

C	A	K	C	O	F	F	E	E	P
J	L	P	C	O	L	A	E	E	E
U	T	A	O	I	C	A	L	E	P
I	I	T	R	R	D	O	T	L	S
C	Z	A	A	E	T	E	A	B	I
E	E	N	C	B	T	T	R	U	T
L	R	G	S	A	E	N	O	N	W
U	L	O	E	J	A	M	I	L	K
I	R	N	B	R	U	B	E	E	R
W	A	T	E	R	G	O	H	A	T

Activity

Place mats

These place mats are easy to make and they look great on the dining table. Cut a piece of thick corrugated card from a cardboard box to the size you want your place mats to be. Stick over this a piece of plain paper in the colour you wish your background to be. Next work your design on this background. You can design a collage of magazine pictures, or use dried leaves or pressed flowers to decorate it. Then you simply cover it with clear, sticky-backed plastic. This allows the place mat to be wiped clean and not get ruined by spillages. This activity is simple and effective and everyone can be included. Try customising the place mats for each person by doing a collage of their favourite things or of pictures they like. This is a good craft to do with people with cognitive impairment, as it enables you to look at and discuss the pictures as you work on the place mat and it requires nothing tricky that the client cannot help with.

This week's excuse for a party!

Race night

PARTY TIME

The idea here is to have a spot of harmless gambling with refreshments. So having had the drinks tasting, get in a supply of the clients' favourites and earlier in the week bake some old-fashioned scones to go with these drinks.

Horse racing is the attraction for the night. You will need six children's toy horses that will stand up, or make six counters out of cardboard and stick a picture of a different horse on each (another excuse for an activity during the week). Tape six sheets of A4 paper end to end to give you a racecourse and divide the racecourse into 50 sections. Place each horse on the starting line and get your clients to place their bets. Then take it in turns to roll the dice for each horse, and repeat until one of the horses crosses the line.

Scones
Mix 8 oz flour and two large pinches of salt in a bowl and then rub in 1½ oz lard. Stir in 1 tbsp sugar and 2 tbsp sultanas. Next, stir in a beaten egg and enough milk to make a soft dough. Roll the dough out half an inch thick and use pastry cutters to make the scones. Brush the tops of the scones with milk and bake at 450°F for about 10 minutes. Serve the scones with strawberry jam and clotted cream or with cheese.

Week 36   September 3–9

Theme
Cakes

Cakes have been around since before the ancient Egyptians – the first
cakes were basically bread sweetened with honey. The word 'cake'
dates back to the thirteenth century and over time cakes became more
sophisticated, with dried fruit and nuts often added. In the
seventeenth century cheap sugar became more available and cakes
evolved into the fancy creations we know today. Ask your clients what
their favourite cakes are. Ask them what the fanciest cake they have
ever eaten was and what was the messiest! Generate a list of as many
cakes as possible, such as Swiss roll, butterfly cake, angel cake and
Battenberg cake. 'Naughty but nice' is a good way of summing up
our relationship with cakes, and while too much may be bad for us
and our cholesterol count … a little of what you fancy does you good!
Ask the group for their memories of their mothers baking cakes. Did
they get to taste the pastry or lick the mixing spoon? Ask the group if
they can remember any recipes of cakes they have made themselves.
Then ask about special cakes such as those for Christmas, weddings
and birthdays. Get members to describe their wedding cakes and the
birthday cakes they made for their children.

Eggless cake
Eggless cake is a Second World War cake designed to save the
rationed eggs for other uses. Mix 1 lb flour and a pinch of salt in a
basin and rub in 4 oz margarine. Stir in 4 oz sugar and 14 oz dried
mixed fruit. Dissolve three saccharin tablets in a tablespoon of hot

water and add this and ½ pint milk and ¼ pint water to the mix and beat well. Bake the cake at 350°F for around 1½ hours.

Basic cupcakes

Here are two different recipes.

1) This recipe is for queen cakes. Beat three eggs and add ½ lb sugar, mixing well. Beat 2 oz butter to a cream and whisk it into the eggs and sugar. Stir in ½ lb flour. Dollop the mixture into cases and bake the queen cakes in a moderate oven.

2) In a warm basin beat 2 oz sugar with 2 oz margarine to make a cream. Stir in 4 oz flour and an egg beaten with 1 tbsp milk. Mix it well. Bake the cupcakes at 425°F for around 15 minutes.

Butterfly cakes

Chop the top off a cupcake and place on it a dollop of buttercream (50 g butter, 100 g icing sugar, 1 tbsp milk). Cut the top of the cupcake in half and set the two pieces standing up in the buttercream so they look like wings!

Activity

Shopping reminiscence

Discuss how prices have changed over the years and how shops have changed from small local grocers and bakers to supermarkets. Ask how people coped before refrigerators and freezers. Talk about modern shopping trends such as late-night and Sunday shopping. A once-a-week drive to the supermarket for groceries to fill up the freezer is often the norm now for working parents, rather than several trips to town throughout the week. Supermarkets often have a bewildering range of choices too, which can make the supermarket an interesting place to go to see what new foods and flavours are available. Ask your clients about stores such as Woolworths where you could by many household essentials in novel ways: biscuits, for example, could be selected from large tins, customers being able to mix and match their favourite ones. The milk delivery has also fallen by the wayside in many areas, but some things are retuning too. Many clients will be able to recall travelling grocery and butchers vans and today many order their shopping online and get it delivered.

This week's excuse for a party!

A cake festival!

A cake festival is not the healthiest of party themes but it is one that will involve clients in its preparation. During the week get a group to bake a basic cupcake mixture, enough to produce three cupcakes per partygoer. Then, working with individuals before party night, help each person to decorate his or her cupcakes. Each person's best cupcake is to be entered into a competition on the night. The other cupcakes are for the communal table at the party. Ingredients that can be used for decorating include icing, food colouring, tubes of coloured icing, coconut, cherries, hundreds and thousands, chocolate buttons, soft sweets and walnuts. On party night the finest cupcakes are displayed on plates alongside the decorator's name and they are then judged for 'Best in Show', second, third, and highly commended (ie the rest). See if you can't get your local baker in to judge the competition. There may be a local college class you could ask to come in and provide a baking demonstration or display. After the competition, bring out the other cupcakes you have made during the week and the tea and sandwiches. Then divide the group into teams and give them the cake quiz.

What does an angel cake do without?
  Egg yolks

Which cake is traditionally pink and yellow and covered in marzipan?
  Battenberg cake

Who wrote the novel Cakes and Ale?
  W Somerset Maugham

What do the French call a cake shop?
  Pâtisserie

What do we call a sponge cake with jam and cream in the middle?
  Victoria cake or sandwich cake

What pastry is long, thin, full of cream and with chocolate on the top?
  Chocolate éclair

Where does the panettone cake come from?
  Italy

What cake has cherries, kirsch and chocolate in it?
  Black Forest gateau

What cake has almonds, raspberry jam and pastry?
  Bakewell tart

Who is the phrase 'Let them eat cake' generally attributed to?
  Marie Antoinette

Week 37   September 10–16

Theme

Bread: the staff of life!

The earliest forms of bread were flatbreads known from over 12,000 years ago and the ancient Egyptians made leavened bread with yeast about 5,000 years ago, often paying their pyramid builders with bread! Bread now exists in a bewildering array of varieties and is a staple foodstuff of many people and cultures. Ask your clients what their favourite type of bread is and if they can remember famous brands such as Hovis, Wonderloaf, Mother's Pride, VitBe and Sunblest. There were also a range of slimming breads popular in the sixties and seventies such as Nimble and Slimcea and slimming crackers such as Ryvita were popular too. Ask clients if they can recall the television advertisements for these and the accompanying slogans. The jingle for Nimble was: 'She flies like a bird in the sky', with pictures of a girl in a hot-air balloon. Slimcea had 'Show them you're a Slimcea girl', and probably the best-known jingle was 'Don't say brown, say Hovis'. Ask people what their favourite sandwiches were and if they ever made their own bread. Then get the group to bake a loaf, because there is nothing quite so nice as the smell of baking bread and the taste of your own loaf!

Basic wartime loaf

Put 2 lb flour into a bowl and mix in 1 tsp sugar, 2 tsp salt and 5 tsp yeast. Sprinkle 1 tbsp vegetable oil over this and pour a pint of warm water into the mixture. Mix this dough well and knead it for about 15 minutes. Put the dough back into the bowl, leave it in a warm place until it has risen to about twice the size, and then knead it again. Divide the dough in two and place in two bread tins dusted with flour. Brush a little water over the top and sprinkle on some rolled oats. Leave the dough for 30 minutes and then bake at 350°F for about 45 minutes.

Milk loaf

Mix 1 lb flour with 1 tsp salt and make into a dough with ½ pint milk. Bake the loaf in a greased tin at about 400°F for an hour.

Lincolnshire plum bread

Many weird and wonderful names and recipes exist for plum bread and this one is an old farm worker's recipe. Rub ½ lb margarine into 2 lb flour and then add ½ tsp salt, 2 lb mixed fruit and 1 lb brown sugar and mix well. Then add 2 tbsp golden syrup, the juice of a lemon and two eggs. Mix to a 'dropping' consistency with a little cold strong tea. Bake the bread at around 300°F for 2–3 hours.

Bread pudding

Take 10 slices of stale bread, soak them in hot water for 10 minutes and then strain out the water through a sieve. Put the bread into a basin and mix in 2 tbsp sugar, 3 tbsp flour, 2 tbsp sultanas, a pinch of salt, 1 tsp baking powder, 1 tsp cinnamon, 2 tbsp margarine and the rind of a lemon. Add just enough milk to make the mixture into a stiff paste and then steam it for 2½ hours. Serve the pudding with custard.

Activity

Types and tasting

The list of speciality breads is staggering. Ask your clients to name as many as they can and write these up on a flip chart. Varieties include soda bread, baguettes, rye bread, wholemeal bread, bagels, ciabatta, croissants, panettone, pumpernickel, pitta, nan, chapattis, crumpets, granary bread, bannock, brioche, muffins, farls and sourdough bread to name just a few! Buy a selection of these from the supermarket and cut them into small squares for people to taste. Have water available, as a bread tasting can make the mouth dry. If favourites emerge be sure to make these a regular feature at mealtimes.

Activity

White powders!

This is an enjoyable sensory test that you can use as a quiz or a perception game. Label some saucers A, B, C, D, E, F, and so on. Upon these put a selection of white or nearly white powders, such as salt, sugar, flour, ground rice, ground coconut, sago, oatmeal, custard powder, cornflour, powdered milk, sherbet, instant potato mix and any others you can think of. The group can then see, feel, smell and taste the powders in order to try to identify them. Give everyone a sheet of paper with the letters of the plates running down the left-hand side, and tell them to write down what they think the powder is on each plate. This is usually very good fun and can be quite difficult. Provide glasses of water, as tasting the powders can make the mouth dry and it is good to have a sip of water in between the different tastes.

This week's excuse for a party!

Murder mystery night!

The date 15 September 1890 saw the birth of one of the greatest crime writers, Agatha Christie. She was the creator of Miss Marple and Poirot, to name just two of her famous characters. So in honour of this you can stage a murder mystery night. From the long list of Agatha Christie films find one that nobody can remember watching. Prepare a buffet supper and then put the film on. At a suitable halfway point, and before it becomes too obvious who the culprit is, ask each person who he or she thinks the perpetrator of the dastardly deed is, and why. Then have your buffet and watch the rest of the film and see who was right. Round the evening off with Miss Marple's favourite tipple: sherry.

Week 38

September 17–23

Theme

Jewish foods

Judaism is one of the oldest religions and one with distinctive customs, traditions, rituals, festivals and foods. Whichever religion or faith clients adhere to, one of the most important ways in which carers can help them to observe their faith is in ensuring they are able to comply with religious food customs. Rosh Hashanah is the Jewish New Year and usually falls somewhere towards the end of September. It is celebrated for 2 days and has special services and prayers. There is a festive meal and 'challah', a special bread, and wine. Honey and other foods are used to symbolise a good omen for the year ahead. So try to visit a kosher shop and try these special foods or ask a Jewish resident or visitor to bring some in for the group. Yom Kippur is celebrated 9 days later and is a day to atone for sins. The day before is considered a festival, with special meals and bread dipped in honey, because on the day itself it is forbidden to eat and drink until the stars come out. Here are some special Jewish foods to try.

Honey cake

Honey cake is traditionally eaten at Rosh Hashanah. Beat three eggs and 1 cup of honey in a bowl. Add a cup of sugar and mix well. Mix into this 1 cup strong black coffee, 1 tbsp baking powder, 1 tsp cinnamon, 1 tsp vanilla essence, 3 tbsp margarine and 4 cups flour. Mix thoroughly and bake in a cake tin at 162°C for an hour.

Tzimmes

Tzimmes is a Rosh Hashanah stew. Heat some vegetable oil in a large pan and add half a dozen sliced carrots and cook for 15 minutes. Add a cubed sweet potato, 4 tsp honey, 4 tbsp sugar, 4 tbsp orange juice, 1 cup dried prunes and a pinch of salt. Cook for 30 minutes.

Hanukkah biscuits

In a bowl, mix 7 oz margarine and 1 cup sugar into a paste. Mix into this two eggs, 3 tbsp orange juice, 1 tbsp vanilla essence and 1 tsp ground cinnamon. Combine 4 oz flour with ½ tsp baking powder and mix this in with the wet mix to make a dough. Put the dough in the fridge for 30 minutes and then roll it out onto a floured surface to biscuit thickness and cut into Hanukkah-themed shapes. Place the biscuits on a greased tray and bake at 425°F for 7 minutes or until they begin to brown.

Apple latkes

Apple latkes are a Hanukkah favourite. Beat two eggs and mix with 1 cup orange juice. In another bowl, mix 8 oz flour with 1 tsp baking powder, a pinch of salt, a pinch of cinnamon and 5 oz sugar. Add the dry mixture to the wet mixture along with three peeled, cored and grated apples and mix well. Drop large spoonfuls of the mixture into hot oil in a pan and fry for about 2 minutes on each side, dry with paper towels and sprinkle with caster sugar.

Activity

Food crossword

This involves making your own crossword. Draw a crossword grid 15 squares by 15 squares and then start filling it in across and down with interlocking food-related words, as shown in the example given here.

	f			p	i	n	e	a	p	p	l e
	l			o							
t	o	m	a	t	o						
	u			a							
c	a	r	r	o	t						
				o							

Keep going until you have squashed as many words in as possible. As an extra activity, transfer this onto a blank grid, black out the unused squares and leave the word squares blank but numbered. Then you have to set about writing the clues. When your crossword is finished, give it to another group or local home to solve and ask them to make one for your group to solve.

Activity

Inter-care home links

It is a good idea to form links with other care homes or goups. The crossword is a good example of an activity that can be shared, and this could develop into regular visits to the other group with games sessions and competitions, and shared parties with either one of the homes or groups preparing and organising to entertain the other to supper or afternoon tea.

This week's excuse for a party!

Jewish night and tasting

Have a selection of baked or bought Jewish foods to try for your Jewish night and tasting, and then try these traditional Jewish games.

Pin the candle on the menorah

This game is like pin the tail on the donkey. Draw the traditional nine-branched candelabrum on a flip chart with the central candle being prominent and give each guest a sticky-backed candle to try to place in the central candleholder while blindfolded.

Find the orange

This is a classic children's party game across cultures and religions, but why let the children have all the fun! Simply ask your clients to leave the room for a moment, hide an orange in the room and then invite the clients back in to try to find it.

Week 39

September 24–30

Theme

Potatoes

For many people the most eaten form of potato is the chip, but many people may not know that chips are not a recent phenomenon. In *A Tale of Two Cities* Charles Dickens writes of 'chips of potatoes fried with … drops of oil'. The first chip shop in the UK is claimed to be in Oldham's Tommyfield Market, where a blue plaque declares that chips were fried there in 1860 – perhaps this was the first fast-food outlet. Ask the group to think about as many different ways of eating potatoes as they can. Apart from chips there are jacket potatoes, mashed potatoes, fried potatoes, boiled potatoes, croquettes, duchesse potatoes, sautéed potatoes and crisps, to name just a few. More inventive wartime recipes included potato soup, stuffed potatoes, potato milk pudding, potato scones and potato chocolate spread! Many were encouraged to grow potatoes during the war years, being informed by the Ministry of Food that potatoes are a good, cheap source of energy and vitamin C, which helps to prevent infection and fatigue. Potatoes also saved on the cost of shipping grain, as they were a substitute for imported cereal crops. Ask the group for their own potato recollections and their favourite potato dishes – for example, bangers and mash or fish and chips. Here are a few other potato dishes to try.

War Ministry potato soup

Slice 1½ lb of unpeeled potatoes, a couple of sticks of celery and a leek (spring onions will do) and drop into 1½ pint salted water and boil until soft. Rub through a sieve or mash very well and add 1 cup milk and reheat. Serve the soup with chopped parsley sprinkled on top.

Crumbed potatoes

Boil new potatoes and then dip them in a beaten egg, roll them in breadcrumbs and fry.

Potato and parsley cakes

Mash 1 lb cold boiled potatoes with 1 oz melted butter. Add 1 tsp chopped parsley, an egg, salt and pepper and mix thoroughly. When the mixture is cool, mould it into small flat cakes. Dip the cakes into beaten egg, roll them in breadcrumbs and then fry them until they are browned.

Stuffed potatoes

Bake some potatoes and then slice off the tops. Spoon out the middle and mash this with chopped parsley and grated cheese. Return the mashed potatoes to the potato shells. Ask the clients for other ideas for fillings.

Potato ribbons

Take a peeled potato and continue to peel it so that you get long, thin, spiral ribbons of potato. Drop the potato ribbons into boiling oil and remove as soon as they begin to change colour.

Potato soufflé

This recipe is from *Foulsham's Universal Cookery Book*. Put 3½ cups warm mashed potato in a saucepan with 1 tbsp butter. Add two egg yolks, 2 tbsp milk, and salt and pepper to taste and stir over heat until well mixed. Remove from the heat and add the two beaten egg whites. Put the potato mixture into a baking dish and brown the top in the oven.

Potato scones

Mix together 6 oz flour, ½ tsp salt, 1 oz sugar and 1 tsp baking powder. Combined this with 4 oz mashed potatoes and rub in 1 oz margarine. Blend the mixture to a dough with a few tablespoons of milk. Roll out the dough and cut it into scone shapes. Brush the tops of the scones with milk and bake them in a hot oven for 15 minutes.

Activity

Labour-saving devices

Did any of the group ever go potato picking? This was a back-breaking task before the invention of machines that do the job. This question might lead into a discussion in general about how machines save us much labour but often at the expense of employment. As regards cookery, there has been an industrial revolution in the kitchen too. We have evolved from open fires to log-burning stoves to gas and electric cookers and microwaves. Now there are many new labour-saving gadgets on the market. Ask your clients to list as many labour savers as they can. These will include the electric tin opener, electric toaster, bread maker, coffee maker, deep-fryer, electric kettle, slow cooker, sandwich toaster, self-cleaning oven, dishwasher, electric whisk, blender, and so on. The easiest labour-saving device, however, is money – then you pay someone else to do it for you! It's a good idea to follow this conversation up with a tasting of some microwaveable foods, such as rice in bags or ready-made lasagne, and see what the clients think of them.

Activity

I went to market

This is a test of memory and a good group game. Sit the group in a small circle and nominate a starter and the direction that you want them to go in around the circle. The idea is members of the group take it in turns to say what they bought at the market, with each person adding another grocery item to the list. For example, 'I went to market and I bought a bunch of bananas', and the next person has to say, 'I went to market and I bought a bunch of bananas and a bag of sugar' and so on until it becomes impossible for one person to remember the entire list. You might need to write the items down, as you will invariably forget too! Once one person has faltered you can try carrying on with the group being allowed to help one another out – it is fun to see how long a list the group can generate with its collective memory. It is surprising just how many list items you can get to.

This week's excuse for a party!

A romantic potato encounter!

There is no such thing as a labour-free party but this romantic potato encounter doesn't take much organisation or preparation. Earlier in the day get the group to prepare a range of easy jacket potato accompaniments and fillings, such as baked beans, grated cheese, a mixed salad, coleslaw, curry, tuna, butter and various sauces. Then sit back and celebrate that on 29 September 1916 the actor Trevor Howard was born. He made many films but he was most famous for his romantic role in *Brief Encounter* with Celia Johnson.

Week 40   October 1–7

Theme

Germany and tea

The date 3 October is German Unity Day, celebrating the unification
of East and West Germany in 1990. The date 3 October 1952 was
also a good day for tea drinkers in the UK, as it was announced by
the Minister of Food that tea rationing was to end. Begin a discussion
by asking your clients for anecdotes about travelling in Germany. It is
a good idea to have some travel brochures to hand to illustrate key
tourist spots. Make a collage while you are doing this around a table
and then discuss the foods and drinks that the clients associate with
Germany. Sour roast, or sauerbraten, is often considered the national
dish, but there are many regional specialities. Sauerbraten is basically
beef marinated in wine or vinegar, beer, juniper berries, onions and
spices and which is then braised in the marinade until it is very
tender. It originated in the ninth century to use up leftover roasts.
The most popular German fast food is the bratwurst sausage, eaten
with mashed potatoes and onions or served in a roll with mustard. It
is also often eaten with sauerkraut, which is sour fermented cabbage.
Two German snacks to make are pretzels and lebkuchen biscuits.

Pretzels

Dissolve 2½ tsp active dry yeast in 6 fl oz warm water. Leave to stand
for 15 minutes and then combine with 1 tsp sugar, ½ tsp salt and
5 oz flour and beat it well. Mix in another 5 oz flour a bit at a time
until you get an elastic dough. Leave the dough in a warm place to
rise and then roll on a floured surface and twist into pretzel shapes.

Brush the dough with a beaten egg, sprinkle with salt and bake at 425°F for about 15 minutes until golden.

Lebkuchen biscuits

Lebkuchen biscuits are ginger-like biscuits traditionally eaten at Christmas. To a bowl add ½ lb brown sugar, 3 oz butter, ½ lb honey and warm it through, stirring. In another bowl mix 8 oz flour, 3 oz ground almonds, 2 tsp ground ginger, 1 tsp baking powder, ⅓ tsp bicarbonate of soda, 1 tsp cinnamon, 1 tsp cloves and the zest of a lemon and an orange. Pour the wet mix into the dry mix and combine until you get a solid dough. Leave the dough to cool. Roll the dough into balls and flatten, and then bake at 356°F for 15 minutes. Make a white icing and use it to decorate the biscuits.

Activity
Tea tasting

To many people there is nothing more welcome in the midst of hard work, and nothing more relaxing, than a cup of tea! However, there is much more to a cup of tea than meets the taste bud. There are many different varieties of tea. The idea here is to have a tea tasting session. A trawl around the local supermarket and delicatessen will unearth many different types and clients can bring in their own too. Some examples are the many different herbal varieties, such as mint and camomile and the more exotic such as chai tea. You can compare the cheapest tea bag with the more expensive types such as Earl Grey – see if you can tell the difference. Try adding lemon or honey to ordinary tea, and have some iced tea, previously prepared, on hand. These will all provide a patchwork of different tastes. You do not want everyone to drink 10 cups of tea in half an hour, so give everyone just a little sample to get the taste. Taste each tea in turn and canvas the opinion of the tasters. Discuss whether milk or sugar should be added or not, and, if milk is added, discuss whether the milk should be added before or after pouring the tea!

Activity

Afternoon tea

Afternoon tea is an essentially English custom, dating from when people traditionally ate their tea later in the evening so it served to bridge the long gap between lunch and dinner. In upper-class circles it became fashionable to turn afternoon tea into a social event, inviting friends along and serving sandwiches, pastries and cakes. Most care homes will have an afternoon tea round, so think about how you can turn this into more of a social event every afternoon. Get people together more and tie it in with a game or quiz so that it becomes a period of socialisation rather than just isolated individuals having a drink on their own. At the very least it should be a focus where staff have a break too and sit down with clients, 'natter' and share a biscuit, not a rushed tea round.

This week's excuse for a party!

Bavarian night

Treat the group to your pretzels and lebkuchen biscuits while holding a German quiz.

What does Apfel mean?   Apple

What is Germany's highest mountain?   Zugspitze (2,962m)

What is bratwurst?   Fried sausage

What is Germany's longest river?   The Rhine

What does Brot mean?   Bread

What do you call traditional German breeches?   Lederhosen

What does Frucht mean?   Fruit

What is the German parliament called?   Bundestag

What does Ober mean?   Waiter

What is Germany's capital city?   Berlin

What does Karotten mean?   Carrots

What used to be Germany's currency?   The deutschmark

What does bitte mean?   Please

What are the colours of the German flag?   Black, red and gold

What does danke mean?   Thank you

What is the famous German Christmas
cake called?   Stollen

What does zwei mean?   Two

What is Germany's national symbol?   A black eagle

What does auf Wiedersehen mean?   Goodbye

What does Volkswagen mean?   People's car

After the quiz try another well-known German favourite, the Black
Forest gateau, and wash this down with some German beer or a fine
sweet white wine such as hock and perhaps a taste of schnapps. A
good way to finish the night is to share some fine German music. Try
Canon in D Major by Johann Pachelbel, Beethoven's Moonlight
Sonata, Bach's 'Air on the G String', and Wagner's 'Ride of the
Valkyries'.

Week 41 October 8–14

Theme

Spain

The date 12 October is Spain's National Day, *Fiesta Nacional de España*, celebrating Christopher Columbus' discovery of America in 1492. Many people will have visited Spain on holiday, as it is one of the most popular package holiday destinations. Indeed, it is so well liked that many 'Brits' retire to its warm climate. Ask around the group for their holiday recollections and if they would like to live in Spain permanently. Make a collage from tourist brochures and use the pictures to stimulate discussion and recall. Explore the pros and cons of this. We often moan about our weather, but what would people miss about the UK if they were to move?

Spain has many regional food specialities but some dishes have become favourites all over Spain and, indeed, the world. Perhaps the best-known Spanish dish is paella, which is basically rice and seafood. Paella originated in the Valencia region of Spain, where meat such as rabbit was mixed with rice and seasonal vegetables. Because of Spain's long Mediterranean coastline, Spain has an abundance of fresh fish and seafood and this has become the main paella meat. Other specialities are Andalusian cold tomato soup, a refreshing summer soup, and the Spanish omelette, made from potatoes and onions.

Paella

This recipe uses Spanish chorizo but you can use any chorizo. Heat 3 tbsp olive oil in a large frying pan or wok. Add a diced onion, a diced red pepper and 220 g sliced chorizo and fry for about 5 minutes. Add

1 tsp turmeric and 300 g of paella or long-grain rice and stir for a minute. Add to this a litre of chicken stock, bring it to the boil and then simmer it for 10 minutes. Stir in two chopped tomatoes, 2 cups defrosted frozen peas and 400 g defrosted mixed frozen seafood. Stir for around 5 minutes more, until the frozen ingredients are cooked through. Squeeze fresh lemon juice over it and serve.

Spanish omelette

Take 1 lb washed unpeeled new potatoes and slice them. Drop them into a frying pan with a chopped onion and a diced red pepper. Cover the vegetables in olive oil and fry gently for about 30 minutes, until the potatoes are soft, and then strain off the oil. Beat six eggs with salt and pepper to taste and a little chopped parsley and mix in the cooked potatoes. Heat some of the oil in a small frying pan and pour in the mixture, cooking it until it is browned underneath. Lower the heat and cover the pan with a lid and cook for another 10 minutes or so until the omelette is set. Alternatively, try sliding the omelette onto a plate and then place another plate over this and turn it over and slide it back in the pan to cook the other side. You can also add grated cheese. Cut the omelette into wedges and eat it either hot or cold.

Andalusian tomato soup (gazpacho)

Take a peeled cucumber, 2 lb ripe, peeled tomatoes, a seeded green pepper, two cloves of garlic, a slice of white bread, ½ cup olive oil, ½ cup red wine vinegar, 2 tsp salt, 1 tsp cumin and 1 cup water and blend until liquidised. Chill in the fridge and serve garnished with croutons and slivers of cucumber.

  Speechmark

Activity

(A)

The local café

Cafés are a good focus for a discussion. Ask your clients about cafés they have used on a regular basis for lunch or on their way to work. Can they remember the older milk bars or the plastic, chrome, tubular steel and Formica tables of the fifties and sixties when jukeboxes began to appear on the scene? There were also many Italian-type cafés springing up in the fifties with espresso coffee machines and frothy cappuccinos. These cafés became very popular with the young as places to 'hang out' and meet, from jazz enthusiasts through to mods, rockers, hippies, punks and beyond. Many of these cafés turned into food outlets in the seventies and eighties but smaller local cafés still exist, so build up a relationship with your local café and use it for quick trips and an excuse for a cup of tea and a piece of cake.

This week's excuse for a party!

Spanish night

PARTY TIME

Hold a Spanish night in honour of Columbus and all things Spanish. Decorate the room with your collage and red and yellow bunting, the colours of the Spanish flag and play flamenco music in the background. After your paella, share a glass of Spanish sherry such as Amontillado or Oloroso and some olives. Another Spanish drink you could make is sangria, which is a wine punch. Just pour a bottle of red wine into a large jug with some ice and some chopped fruit of your choice and add a bottle of lemonade. Then sit back and try this Spanish quiz.

What is Spain's capital?
  Madrid

Spain is separated from France by which mountain range?
  The Pyrenees

Famous Spanish cubist artist, Pablo who?
  Picasso

What is a toro?
  Bull

What is Spain's old unit of currency?
  Peseta

What is the Spanish name for Spain?
  España

Where was the painter El Greco born?
  Crete

Which large Mediterranean island group is part of Spain?
  Canary Islands

What is a burro?
  Donkey

Name a donkey-riding hero of Spanish literature.
  Don Quixote

What is Spain's major religion?
  Roman Catholicism

What is the national football stadium in Madrid called?
  The Estadio Santiago Bernabéu

What do we call Spanish traditional dancing?
  Flamenco

What is Spain's national flower?
  Red carnation

Who was the Nationalist leader in the Spanish Civil War?
  General Franco

What is Gaudi's Barcelona cathedral commonly known as?
  La Sagrada Familia

What is the 'wild coast' north of Barcelona called?
  Costa Brava

Which palace overlooks Granada?
  Alhambra

Rossini's famous opera is The Barber of …?
  Seville

What is the Spanish pure-bred horse called?
  The Andalusian

Week 42 October 15–21

Theme

Kitchens, cookers and gadgets

Throughout our lives we spend a lot of time in our kitchens and these have changed over the years, as has the equipment we use in them. So ask the group to recall their childhood kitchens, cookers and gadgets and memories of helping their mother bake and cook. Can people remember their grandparents' houses and kitchens and did any cook on a cast-iron range? Gone is the pantry, replaced by the fridge-freezer. Gone is the glass milk bottle, and the handle-operated handheld whisk has been replaced by an electric version. Ask your clients what other devices and gadgets have disappeared. Can they remember the Tupperware era and the dawn of the electric toaster? Does anyone remember toasting bread in the fire on a long fork? Such apparatuses as pressure cookers have become smaller and more efficient than the huge heavy ones of the past – they used to whistle and steam as if they were going to explode. Did people have liquidisers and early food mixers? Think about storage too – what sort of cupboards were used for the pots, plates and pans and did they have bread bins and biscuit barrels? Did anyone have a Welsh dresser, a lazy Susan or a hostess trolley? Did people wear pinafores? Here is a list of kitchen utensils that may trigger memories and discussion as to their ease of use and worth! Potato peeler, corkscrew, egg slicer, egg timer, cheese grater, lemon squeezer, food slicer, mincer, nutcrackers, potato masher and can opener. Also, ask if anyone ever had a dishwasher, and give bonus points for the answer 'husband'!

Family recipes were often handed down the generations by word of mouth, and while they date back to the Roman Empire it was not until the eighteenth century that recipe books began to appear en masse. The year 1861 saw the first *Mrs Beeton's Book of Household Management* published and this led the way for many other domestic service manuals and cookery books. Ask clients about their family recipes and cookery books they have used. Try to get a few older recipe books to pass around. Get some brochures from the local kitchen superstore too, in order to show the latest modern kitchens to contrast with the reminiscences of kitchens past.

Activity
Instant food

No need for recipes this week. Just take a stroll around the supermarket with the group looking at instant meals. Some will be microwaveable, others oven baked and some tinned. These meals are very convenient and can be nutritious, such as beans on toast. Look too for instant puddings and instant cake mixes and buy a selection to make and try. The obvious question then is, are they as good as home-made cakes?

Activity
Gadget guess

For this activity you need a range of kitchen, baking and cookery equipment. For obviously recognisable items place each one inside a cardboard box and seal it. The box is then passed around and people have to guess what is in it. The clues are in its weight and the noise it makes as you shake the box. For more unusual items place these inside a pillowcase and tie it up. With these, people can feel the shape and outline of the object as well as its weight.

Activity

Twenty uses for a ...

Pick a kitchen utensil such as a fish slice and pass it around the group. Then ask the group to come up with 20 different uses for the kitchen utensil. Write the uses down on a flip chart as they get called out. If it proves too easy, make it 50 uses.

Activity

Kitchen porter

This activity calls for not exactly a kitchen porter but rather a kitchen helper and tidier. There are a thousand and one jobs about the kitchen that could be done by an enthusiastic client working in co-operation with the cook. There will be things that can be done to assist with the preparation of food on a daily basis. There will also be jobs centred on keeping the place clean and tidy that can be done on a weekly if not a daily basis. It would be easy to work with your cook to come up with a daily or weekly schedule of jobs in which people could be involved. There will also be major kitchen tasks every now and again, such as a thorough clean, of the 'behind the cooker' variety. The cupboards will need to be completely cleared and cleaned every so often, and the cutlery and crockery should be inspected on a regular basis for defects and cleanliness. Such a role may be perfect for many clients who have had a life of domesticity and who find it hard not to be involved any more.

Speechmark

Activity

More food-related proverbs and colloquialisms

- It's just sour grapes

- He's bought a lemon

- Out of the frying pan into the fire

- Don't count your chickens before they have hatched

- You don't miss the water until the well runs dry

- An apple a day keeps the doctor away

- Live from hand to mouth

- Chewing the fat

- Put through the mill

- Butter wouldn't melt in her mouth

- Mutton dressed as lamb

- Keen as mustard

- Easy as pie

- In the soup

This week's excuse for a party!

Labour-saving party

The best way to do this is to persuade someone to come in and prepare, run and clear up a party for you. While the likelihood of this is probably slim, a sort of halfway house might be to just go to the supermarket and buy readymade snacks, letting the clients choose for themselves something savoury and sweet. Then sit back and watch a film. Rita Hayworth was born on 17 October in 1918, so ask the clients which of her films they can remember. Many were memorable but her best were reputedly *Miss Sadie Thompson*, *Gilda*, *Blood and Sand*, *You Were Never Lovelier* and *Cover Girl*.

Week 43 October 22–28

Theme:

School dinners and Diwali

This week is a good time to find out more about the Hindu festival of Diwali, which usually falls in October or November in the English calendar. Alongside this we look back this week at the delights of school meals and packed lunches.

School meals

Begin a discussion by asking your clients for recollections of their school meals. Did they like school meals or not and do they have memories of particular favourite meals or puddings, or meals they hated? Explore the dubious delights of lumpy mashed potato, watery custard and teachers patrolling up and down to ensure you ate all your greens. Some will have taken a packed lunch instead, and most of us will have had packed lunches in our working lives, so ask what different things people used to take. Did people use a flask for hot tea? It always seems to taste better if you are working outside or on a walk. Ask about work canteens too and what these were like. Back at school, do people remember free school milk and was it kept cold or did it get warm and unpleasant? Did anyone have the job of milk monitor?

Diwali

This is the Hindu 'festival of lights' and it is good to know something about it if you are not Hindu yourself. The date is set by the Hindu calendar and so it changes every year according to the position of the moon. It is one of the most important festivals, being the Hindu New

Year. The lamps and lights of the festival symbolise the lifting of spiritual darkness and the victory of good over evil. In India, oil lamps are floated on the Ganges. Apart from the lamps, homes are decorated and sweets are made, so of course it is popular with children. The festival lasts for 5 days and there are many Hindu legends and tales surrounding the festival. Try to get some of the decorated sweets to taste or make them using the recipes given here. Try inviting members of the local Hindu community to come in to talk about the festival. The festival also celebrates a successful harvest and new clothes are worn and the house is cleaned to welcome the new year. Windows are opened to let in Lakshmi, the goddess of wealth – she cannot enter a dark house, hence the lamps, which are said to light the way for her. Another story tells of a princess, Sita, kidnapped by an evil king. She left a trail of jewellery so that her husband, Rama, could find her. Rama was helped by all the animals in the world and the King was killed – the festival celebrates this triumph of good over evil.

Diwali snacks

You will need some special ingredients for Diwali snacks, but these can be easily sourced from specialist or Indian food shops or on the internet.

Coconut burfi

Fry a handful of broken cashew nuts in 1 tbsp ghee and put to one side. Heat 1 cup grated coconut and 1 cup sugar in the pan until the sugar melts and becomes syrupy. Add the cashews, a pinch of edible camphor and 1 tbsp cardamom powder. Stir for a few minutes until the sugar crystallises and begins sticking to the sides of the pan. Spread the mixture onto a greased tray and cut it into shapes while it is still warm. For a chocolate alternative, mix 2 tsp cocoa powder in when you add the cashews.

Rava laddu

Heat ¼ cup ghee and roast a handful of broken cashews in a frying pan. Remove the cashews and add 1 cup semolina (rava) to the ghee and roast it. Take it off the heat before it browns, set it aside and allow it to cool. Grind the roasted rava to a powder and mix with ¾ cup sugar in a bowl. Add the cashews and 1 tsp cardamom powder. Then heat up the ghee and add it to the dry mixture, combining well until it resembles bread, and then form the mixture into bite-sized balls. You can roll these in coconut and add cocoa powder for a chocolate version and place an almond on the top.

Chocolate pedas

Mix 2 tbsp cocoa powder, 4 tbsp milk powder, 3 tbsp powdered almonds, and four powdered rich tea-type biscuits with a few tablespoons of boiled milk to make a dough. With oiled hands, form the dough into balls. Again, you can roll these in coconut and put an almond on top.

Sandesh (cheesy fudge)

Boil 1¾ pints milk and add 2 tbsp lemon juice. As the milk curdles stir it continuously. Water will separate and should be strained off, leaving what is called 'paneer', which is hung in a muslin bag to drain for 30 minutes or so. Wash it and squeeze out the water again and then add 1 cup powdered sugar and grind it into a smooth paste. Heat this in a frying pan for 10 minutes and add a few small strands of saffron and continue to heat until it loses its stickiness. Form it into balls and push a dent in the top of each ball with your thumb and garnish the balls with crushed pistachios. These sweets will harden as they cool.

Activity

Diwali candles and glass painting

The idea here is to make salt dough diwas or lamps that can hold tea lights. To make the salt dough, mix 1 cup salt to 2 cups flour and 1 cup water. Make the dough into balls, flatten the balls and shape them into bowls with a pointed spout at on end. Bake the bowls for an hour until they are hard. These can then be painted and decorated with sequins, beads and glitter – the brighter the better. Then drop a tea light into each one and light them. Another good idea is to get a glass-painting kit and decorate small glass jars and put tea lights in these.

This week's excuse for a party!

Diwali

Putting it all together, light all the candles and bring out all the Diwali snacks and sit down to watch the film *Slumdog Millionaire*.

Week 44 — Oct 29–Nov 4

Theme

Halloween

The date 31 October is Halloween. It is also called All Hallows' Eve, as it is the day before All Saints' Day and 2 days before All Souls' Day, when it was customary to pray for the dead, hence the association with death. Over 2000 years ago this was New Year for the Celts who burned bonfires to try to keep evil spirits away. Ask your clients how they used to celebrate Halloween. Did they wear fancy dress and go 'trick-or-treating'? Did they carve pumpkins and light a candle inside? In keeping with the Halloween theme, ask the clients what was the scariest thing that ever happened to them and what was the scariest film they have ever seen. Follow this with a discussion as to what is the best ghost story or horror story they have read. Halloween is big business these days and it is even more celebrated in the United States. The baking of special Halloween cakes and the preparation of Halloween party food gives you some good shared activity, such as baking small cupcakes and decorating them with spiders, pumpkin faces, ghosts, and the like.

Pumpkin pie

Roll out 9 oz shortcrust pastry and line a pie tin with it, pricking the base with a fork. Brush with a beaten egg and bake at 375°F for 30 minutes. Boil 12 oz seeded pumpkin in lightly salted water for 15 minutes, then strain, blend and cool it. Mix this with two eggs and 2 oz brown sugar, 2 fl oz double cream and 1 tsp ground cinnamon. Fill the pastry case with the mixture and bake at 375°F for 40 minutes.

Activity

Autumn foraging

Because it's autumn and the season for fruits, it's a good time to go foraging in the local woods. There are many things you can pick, such as brambles, in order to give your walk an extra purpose besides fresh air, exercise and just enjoying the countryside and autumn colours. Many used to make their own jam from the fruits of the field, so here is an old traditional recipe to try.

Sloe and apple jam

Pick and dry 4 lb sloes. Peel, core and quarter 4 lb sweet apples. Boil the peelings with just enough water to cover until all the goodness is extracted, and then strain off the juice. Put the sloes, apples and juice into a preserving pan or large saucepan and cook until the fruit is soft. Allow it to cool and then rub it through a sieve. Return the pulp to the pan and add 6 lb sugar and the rind and juice of two lemons and boil, stirring all the time for about 15 minutes. Pour the jam into pots and seal and allow to set.

This week's excuse for a party!

Halloween

If the clients are willing, make it a fancy (horror) dress Halloween party. This will give you many opportunities for group and one-to-one activity in preparation work and costume making. One of the obvious ways to make the party that bit more special at Halloween is to carve a pumpkin and put a candle light inside it. This is easy once you have tried it, and clients can either do it themselves or simply advise about the design. However, caution must be taken because you will need sharp knives, as the pumpkins are quite tough. Basically, you just cut off the top of the pumpkin and keep it to form the lid. Then you scoop out all the seeds and stringy bits in the centre of the pumpkin. This will leave you with a hollow pumpkin with walls about 3–4 cm thick. Draw your fierce face design on the pumpkin shell and then cut it out. All you need to do then is pop in a night light, light it and replace the lid. A few of these pumpkins will look good on the party tables. Do not throw away the pumpkin pips – try growing them in pots indoors and if it works, plant them out later.

To give your party a bit more of a Halloween flavour, try a game of pumpkin quoits. You will need six small pumpkins and six rings that will fit over the pumpkins – these can be made from thick cardboard. Spread the pumpkins out and write a score on each one, and then get the clients to have turns at throwing the rings over the pumpkins. Apple bobbing is another traditional game at this time of year. If you don't want to get wet, then just hang the apples with string from the ceiling and try to get a bite into one. It is not so easy! If it is a fine night you could go outside for a round or two of 'Tossing the Pumpkin', whereby each player gets several attempts to toss a fairly hefty pumpkin as far as they can. Another good idea is to round off the party with a good horror film. So get the clients to discuss these options and vote for one beforehand.

Week 45　　　　November 5–11

Theme

Bonfire Night and Poland

The date 5 November 1605 was the day Guy Fawkes was arrested trying to blow up the Houses of Parliament. Since then, Bonfire Night has become one of the UK's main festivals. The date 11 November is National Independence Day in Poland, commemorating the restoration of Polish independence after the First World War. It is a national holiday celebrated with family get-togethers, meals and fireworks.

Bonfire Night

Bonfire Night or Guy Fawkes is a major event for children in the UK, with fireworks and 'guys' burned on bonfires. Before being burned, however, the guy earns his fire by being wheeled around the neighbourhood in an old 'pram' with children asking a 'penny for the guy'. After some pennies have been amassed, the children rush to the local shops and buy sweets or 'bangers'. Mischief Night is another tradition, involving playing tricks on your neighbours such as knocking on the door and running away. Another tradition, and a necessary one for England, is the habit of wrapping potatoes up in tinfoil and placing them in the fire to cook. These certainly warm you up on a cold November night. Ask your clients for their Bonfire Night recollections. Did they have any favourite fireworks, such as Catherine wheels and rockets? The best way of sparking some recall and the best trigger you could have would be to have your own fireworks display. Clients can be involved in the preparation of food and drinks and can help to make the guy for the bonfire, and don't forget the sparklers. A good activity is to get the clients to make their own guy from old clothes stuffed with newspaper!

Bonfire toffee

Put 12 oz dark brown sugar, 4 oz butter, 2 tbsp golden syrup, 2 tbsp molasses and 4 tbsp water into a pan and heat until the sugar has dissolved. Boil the mixture, stirring it occasionally, until it solidifies when you drop a bit in cold water – usually 20–40 minutes. Pour the mixture into a buttered tray and leave it to set. When the toffee is hard, break it up with a hammer.

Polish food

Invite the group's recollections of Poland and their Polish friends. Many Polish pilots flew with the Royal Air Force in the Second World War and so, as a result of the ties they made, many Polish people settled in the UK. These people brought with them some aspects of their national cuisine. A traditional meat stew called 'bigos' is considered to be the national dish and there is no one recipe, just many family variations. Bigos typically has cabbage, meats, often sausage, tomatoes, mushrooms and honey and it is heavily seasoned with herbs including juniper. It used to be traditional at holiday times to keep a big pot of bigos on the go for a week, replenishing the ingredients as you needed them. Polish meals often start with soup, and beetroot soup is a particular Polish speciality.

Beetroot soup

Beetroot soup is an easy and warming soup ideal for Bonfire Night. Fry a chopped onion and a clove of garlic in olive oil until soft. Add three large peeled and chopped beetroots and after a couple of minutes add a pint of beef or chicken stock. Add salt and black pepper to taste and three sliced carrots. Bring the soup to the boil and simmer it for 30 minutes. Remove the soup from heat, put it through a blender, reheat it and serve it with a swirl of cream or yoghurt on top.

Stuffed cabbage

Take a large cabbage and boil it until the outer leaves soften and start to fall away. Take the cabbage out of the water and remove these outer leaves and set them aside. Re-boil the cabbage and repeat this process until you have all the leaves. Remove any large stalks from the centres of the leaves. Fry a diced onion in butter for a few minutes. Mix this in a bowl with 1½ lb minced meat and ½ lb cooked rice and one egg. Add salt, pepper and seasonings of your choice such as parsley. Divide this mixture into portions, shape these portions into rolls and wrap the rolls in cabbage leaves to make parcels. Place these parcels into a casserole dish, making sure any leaf joins are face down to stop the parcels unrolling. Pour over the parcels a sauce of your choice or use a tin of chopped tomatoes seasoned with salt and pepper and a little stock. Bake for 1½ hours at 350°F.

This week's excuse for a party!

Fireworks with hot potatoes

Organise your own firework display and bonfire. Start with your beetroot soup and then burn the clients' guy and set off the fireworks. Don't forget the sparklers! Try baking some jacket potatoes on the fire too and eat your bonfire toffee. Combining this week's two themes, people might like to try a small glass of traditional Polish fruit-flavoured vodka to warm them up, but don't stand too close to the bonfire!

Activity

Post-bonfire photo rocket

Make sure you take a camera out with you on Bonfire Night and take pictures of the clients in the glow of the fire. Try to get good close-ups of people's faces. Then make a rocket out of rolled-up cardboard. Paint it bright colours and place a stick coming out of the rear with some red and yellow tissue paper to represent rocket flames. This is then hung horizontally from the ceiling and from this at varying heights you hang a series of photographs from the night. Stick the photographs back to back so that as they spin around you get two images. This rocket will remind clients of the night and it will also be visually stimulating to watch.

Week 46 November 12–18

Theme

Cheese and Ramadan

Cheese is an important part of people's diet all over the world, so this week we focus on the vast range of different cheeses and the versatility of cheese. Ramadan is one of the main Muslim festivals. Ramadan can occur anywhere in the year, as it is set according to the lunar calendar, but we will examine it in this week.

Cheese

Start by brainstorming all the different types of cheese the clients can think of and write each type down on a flip chart – it's surprising just how many there are. Get each member to tell the group what their favourites are and then ask them to think of all the different ways there are to eat cheese and all the different recipes they can remember – generate a list of favourites. The best way to follow this brainstorm session up is to hold a cheese tasting. So have a good selection of world cheeses in small pieces on plates to pass around. Include famous British cheeses too, such as Wensleydale, Cheddar, Caerphilly and Stilton. Each person can then comment upon the taste and texture and whether or not they like it. Have glasses of water available to refresh the palate between cheeses. Remember to record individual clients' favourites so you can ensure that the clients get their favourites every now and then. Ask the clients for their recollections of baking with cheese, because during rationing in the Second World War many inventive ways were found of using the precious weekly ration of 2 oz per person. There was even a Ministry of Food 'War Cookery Leaflet No 12' dedicated to cheese. This leaflet extolled the virtues of cheese for bones, teeth and muscles – indeed, cheese is a good source of protein and calcium. One rather unhealthy suggestion in the same leaflet is 'cheese frizzles'.

Cheese frizzles

Mix together 2 tbsp oatmeal, 1 tbsp flour, 2 tbsp grated cheese and a little salt and pepper. Add a little cold water to make a batter and mix in 1 tsp baking powder. Drop spoonfuls of the mixture into hot fat and fry them on both sides until browned.

BeRo cheese fingers

Mix 8 oz flour with a pinch of salt and rub in 3 oz margarine. Then mix in 3 oz grated cheese, a beaten egg and 1 tbsp milk. Roll the dough out into a long, thin roll and cut it into finger lengths. Prick the lengths with a fork and bake them at 350°F for 20 minutes.

Browned cheese carrots

Cut carrots into thin slices lengthwise and boil them for 15 minutes. Drain them and place them in a well-greased dish. Cover the carrots with grated cheese and brown them under the grill.

Ramadan

The Muslim festival of Ramadan is based upon the lunar calendar and as such the dates for the festival tend to move each year. Ramadan is a month of fasting between dawn and sunset. It is not commercialised and it is about self-sacrifice and devotion to Allah. Bits of the Koran are recited each night in many mosques so that by the end of the month all of the Koran has been read. The fasting means that you are not allowed to eat or drink while the sun shines – this serves to remind people of the poor. The holiday Eid ul-Fitr marks the end of Ramadan and is celebrated with a feast.

Carrot halwa cake

Mix together 2 cups flour and 3 tsp baking powder. In another bowl mix 2½ cups shredded carrot, ½ cup raisins, 4 tbsp sugar, ½ cup milk and 2 cups condensed milk. Microwave this for about 7 minutes on high and mix in ½ cup unsalted butter. Mix this in with the flour mixture, along with a pinch of ground nutmeg and six crushed cardamom seeds. Spread the mixture onto a greased baking tray and bake it at 176°C for around 20 minutes. Sprinkle icing sugar over the top and add some flaked almonds and cranberries.

Activity

Edible cracker art!

Have ready a plate for each client, and place dishes with sliced, cottage and cream cheese peanut butter, various jams, pickles and spreads in the centre of the table. Also have dishes with lots of extra accompaniments such as cooked prawns, sliced cucumber, sliced tomato, spring onion rings, radishes, olives, sliced apple, sliced strawberry, sliced banana and carrot slivers. There is an almost limitless number of ways of garnishing a cracker. Now, the clients have a plain square cracker each and are in competition to win the best-decorated and tastiest cracker prize.

This week's excuse for a party!

Cheese, wine and Wallace party!

Supper is a cheese and wine party with a range of different crackers, spreads and toppings and a wide range of the world's cheeses. There should be wine for accompaniment alongside non-alcoholic choices. This is a good event to invite family and friends to. Form the group into teams and try to answer these cheese questions.

What is the French for fresh cheese?
  Fromage frais

What kind of cheese is made backwards?
  Edam (m-a-d-e)

What is the most popular cheese in Greece?
  Feta

What cheese comes from buffalo milk?
  Mozzarella

Spell mozzarella
  M-o-z-z-a-r-e-l-l-a

What is Wallace and Gromit's favourite cheese?
  Wensleydale

Stilton can only be made in three counties: Derbyshire, Nottinghamshire and ...?
  Leicestershire

What type of milk is Roquefort cheese made from?
  Sheep milk

Where does Gruyère cheese come from?
  Switzerland

Spell Gruyère
  G-r-u-y-è-r-e

Where does Parmesan cheese come from?
  Italy

What is Welsh rarebit?
  Cheese on toast

Where does Camembert come from?
  France

What is the Italian word for cheese?
  Formaggio

What do we call melted cheese that you dip food into?
  Fondue

Tot up the scores and round the night off with a 'nice piece of Wensleydale' and a screening of a Wallace and Gromit animation.

Week 47 November 19–25

Theme

Baking and Thanksgiving

Baking

While these days baking seems to be a dying art, with people seemingly being too busy to bake, many clients will have been bakers themselves or will be able to recall their mothers baking for the home. Were they allowed to help and did they get to dip their fingers into the cake mix? Children often baked cakes at school too. In many households, just as washing day was a Monday, baking was also carried out on the same day each week, as was the weekly 'town' shop, usually market day. So discuss you clients' talents and memories. Have a few old baking recipe books to hand and some older utensils such as a hand whisk, old scales and cake cases to stimulate discussion. Group members might have their favourite recipes, which you could help them to bake. The old cookery books such as *Foulsham's Universal Cookery Book* and *Be-Ro Home Recipes* also gave tips for the home baker as well as recipes, and it would be good to see if the bakers in the group agree with some of these tips, or if they have tips of their own to share. These words of wisdom include 'never allow margarine to "oil"!', 'dip your spoon in milk before spooning a mixture into cake cases, as this stops the mixture sticking to the spoon' and finally, 'do not shut the oven door with a bang'!

Try making a selection of jam and lemon tarts with a simple pastry such as 8 oz flour and two pinches salt mixed together and blended with 4 oz margarine, 1 oz sugar and enough water to make a dough.

NOVEMBER

Here are a few old baking recipes to try out.

Maids of honour

Cream 2 oz margarine with 2 oz sugar. Mix in 1 oz desiccated coconut, a beaten egg and the juice of half a lemon. Line tart tins with the pastry and half-fill them with the mixture. Bake the tarts at 400°F for around 15 minutes.

Fruit scones

Mix 8 oz flour with two pinches of salt and rub in 1½ oz hard margarine. Mix into this 1 tbsp sugar and 2 tbsp sultanas, and then add a beaten egg and enough milk to form the mixture into a dough. Shape the mixture into scones, brush the tops with beaten egg and bake them at 450°F for 10 minutes.

Rock cakes

Rub 3 oz margarine into ½ lb flour and then mix in 2 oz caster sugar, 2 oz currants and a little nutmeg. Combine the mixture with one egg and a little milk. Drop dollops onto a greased baking tray. Baste each dollop with egg white and sprinkle brown sugar over them. Bake the rock cakes at 400°F for around 15 minutes.

Melting moments

Blend together 4 oz margarine, 1 tsp vanilla essence, 3 oz caster sugar and an egg. Mix into this 5 oz flour. Form the mixture into balls and roll them in oats and then flatten. Bake the biscuits at 350°F for 20 minutes. Decorate each with half a glacé cherry.

Thanksgiving

Thanksgiving is always on the fourth Thursday in November and is primarily a North American celebration. Ask if any group members have visited the United States or Canada and get them to describe their trips. Thanksgiving is similar to our harvest festival but there are big parades and family get-togethers. A roast turkey is traditionally the centrepiece of a family dinner and is eaten with cranberry sauce. As at Halloween, pumpkin pie is often eaten as a dessert. Ask group members about our own harvest festivals and decorating the church with flowers and produce. November has always been a time for celebrating the harvest and marking the beginnings of winter. Many superstitious customs and practices abound at this time of year as it becomes darker earlier. In the old days people used to believe the Devil was a nut gatherer, so they would wear hazel nuts as magic charms! There was also much bell-ringing, dancing and merrymaking as the grape harvest was put to test! What superstitions have the clients heard of?

Activity
Kim's food game

This game is sometimes called the memory tray. It is good fun and tests our powers of recall. The degree of difficulty is easily varied, making it easy to adapt for any group. You need a selection of food-related items such as vegetables, a fork, a salt cellar, a sweet and, of course, a tray. Use 20 items for a difficult game and 10 for a much easier one. After a couple of games you will know what number is about right for your group. Place the items on the tray out of sight of the group and cover it with a pillowcase, and then lay the tray on the floor in the middle of the group. Explain to the group that you are going to uncover the tray for a while and that you want them to take a good look at all the items. A slow count of ten is about right before you place the pillowcase back over the tray. The group then has to

NOVEMBER

remember what was on the tray. Get them to shout out the items while you record their responses on a flip chart. When they have exhausted their memories, reveal the contents again for them to see if they have got them all. A good idea is to follow this with another activity and at the end ask them again what was on the tray. Alternatively, get them together again later in the day and ask them. Remember to use items the group members can recognise.

This week's excuse for a party!

Harvest festival

Get the clients to make a church harvest festival type display in a room corner and then decorate the supper table in a similar manner. Add to this the fruits of their baking skills, carefully arranged as if they were going to be judged at a village fete. Then prepare two bowls of fruit punch, one with a bottle of sparkling wine and one alcohol-free. Garnish these with fruits such as chopped grapefruit, halved grapes, mandarin segments and a few cherries. This is a good event to invite family and friends to so that they can admire the display and the baking.

Week 48　　Nov 26 – Dec 2

Theme

Scotland

The date 30 November is St Andrew's Day. St Andrew is the patron saint of Scotland, so this is a good week to taste things Scottish such as whisky and haggis! Ask your clients for their memories of visiting Scotland and whether anyone has ever seen the Loch Ness monster! Use this as a springboard to generate a list on a flip chart of all things Scottish, such as heather, thistles, tartan, lochs, the Highlands, snow and midges. Get a few travel and tourist brochures to act as triggers and make a Scottish-themed collage. Then try to think about different types of Scottish food and drink such as shortbread, whisky and haggis. People have inhabited Scotland since around 7,000 BC and the cuisine has many Irish and Scandinavian influences. Oats and barley were crofters' staples, and porridge was a much-used food, which, as well as being eaten boiled with milk, served to make cakes and bannocks too. The cauldron hanging over an open fire was the usual method of cooking with whichever meat and vegetables could be had. Scotland is now famed for its beef, salmon and venison, as well as its haggis. Haggis is sheep offal minced and mixed with suet, oatmeal and seasoning, which is then stuffed and sewn into a sheep's stomach lining. Here are some other famous Scottish dishes to try.

Neeps and tatties

Neeps and tatties are basically potatoes and swedes boiled, mashed and buttered. It is a traditional accompaniment to haggis.

Shortbread

Shortbread used to be an expensive treat for the poor. It is traditionally eaten on New Year's Day and was a favourite of Mary, Queen of Scots. Mix 3 oz caster sugar in a bowl with 5 oz cold butter. Mix in 6 oz plain flour, 2 oz rice flour and a pinch of salt. Knead the mixture into a stiff dough, roll it out and shape it as required. Prick the shortbread with a fork and then bake at 300°F for around 35 minutes. Another, much simpler, 1940s recipe uses only ¼ lb margarine, ½ lb flour and 2 oz sugar. Mix the ingredients thoroughly, roll out the dough, cut it with pastry cutters and prick it with a fork. Bake the shortbread in a 'moderate' oven until light brown.

Cullen skink

Cullen skink is a traditional fish soup. Cover 12 oz skinned haddock with boiling water and keep it boiling. Add a chopped onion and simmer the soup for 10 minutes. Drain the pot and reserve the liquid. Flake the fish and remove any bones. Strain the liquid into a pint of milk, bring to the boil and then simmer for an hour. Cook and mash 1½ lb potatoes with some butter. Add the fish and potatoes to the liquid. Serve the soup with chopped parsley.

Dundee cake

Mix 6 oz margarine with ¾ lb brown sugar and then mix in three beaten eggs and ½ lb flour. Next, mix in ½ lb rice flour and ¼ pint milk. Mix thoroughly, adding 1 tsp baking powder, ½ lb raisins, ¼ lb sultanas and 2 tbsp candied peel. Bake the cake in a greased tin at 350°F for 2½ hours or so.

Activity

Scottish quiz

What is the capital of Scotland?

Edinburgh

Where is Scotland's 'monster' found?

Loch Ness

Which Scot invented television?

John Logie Baird

What is Edinburgh's volcano called?

Arthur's Seat

What famous New Year song did Robert Burns write?

'Auld Lang Syne'

What is a Munro?

A Scottish mountain

Which Scot invented the telephone?

Alexander Graham Bell

What is the highest mountain in the British Isles called?

Ben Nevis

Who is celebrated on 25 January?

Robert Burns

What village is famous for runaway marriages?

Gretna Green

What do we call a kilt's pouch?

Sporran

Where are the 'bonnie, bonnie banks'?

Loch Lomond

What oatmeal breakfast did the Scots invent?

Porridge

Which Scottish city is also known as the Granite City?

Aberdeen

What is Scotland's national stadium called?

Hampden Park

What is 'uisge beatha', or the water of life?

Whisky

The MacDonalds and Campbells were involved in which massacre?

The Massacre of Glencoe

What is an Arbroath smokie?

A smoked haddock

Name the Highland sport, tossing the …

Caber

Name a traditional Scottish musical wind instrument.

The bagpipes

This week's excuse for a party!

Scottish night

A Scottish night could include haggis, shortbread and whisky tasting, and the men could all wear kilts and bagpipe music could be played. Try to get a local dance society or college group to come in to give a demonstration of traditional Scottish dancing. Get them to teach you all a few basic steps and then have a go. Try out the Highland fling and the Gay Gordons, which is an old-time social dance for partners where every couple dances the same steps in a circle around the room. It is named after the Scottish regiment the Gordon Highlanders and is popular at ceilidhs. Try the Scottish quiz and end the night with a whisky toast. If a film is requested then perhaps *Whisky Galore!* would be a good choice.

Week 49　　　　　　December 3–9

Theme

Alcohol

The date 5 December 1933 saw the end of Prohibition in the United States. Alcohol comes in many varieties and it is this diversity that is the focus this week. This makes for an interesting discussion in relation to people's drinking habits. Alcohol can play a large part in people's social lives, whether it is a regular evening in the local pub or sharing a bottle of wine with friends over a meal. One good way to start the discussion is by asking people what their favourite drinks are and then list the names of as many different drinks they can remember. Examples might include Watneys Red Barrel, Babycham, Guinness, Cherry B and snowballs. Many of these were party or Christmas drinks. Ask about the occasions people have had champagne and of any strange drinks they have tried, such as exotic cocktails or drinks from abroad. Can people remember going to parties as teenagers and taking those Party Seven tins of beer? Ask if people can remember the commercial advertising slogans such as 'Guinness is good for you' and 'Double Diamond works wonders'. Another important aspect of the discussion of course is to ask about hangover cures! Here is a recipe for a healthy drink that will aid the recovery process!

Healthy drink

Take two carrots, 2 tbsp honey, 2 L fresh orange juice and some ice cubes. Put the carrots and the honey into a blender, mix and then add the ice cubes and orange juice. Blend it all again. Serve this in a glass with a fruit slice over the rim and a straw. Add a cocktail umbrella to make it look exotic! Experiment with the carrots until you get the consistency and taste you like.

Activity

Drinking quotations

Water, water, every where,
Nor any drop to drink.

Samuel Taylor Coleridge

Let us have wine and women, mirth and laughter,
Sermons and soda water the day after.

Lord Byron

Abstainer: a weak person who yields to the temptation of denying himself a pleasure.

Ambrose Bierce

Drink because you are happy, but never because you are miserable.

GK Chesterton

[He] finished his half-pint … with the slowness of a man unable to see where the next was coming from.

WW Jacobs

Much drinking, little thinking.

Jonathan Swift

I cook with wine, sometimes I even add it to the food.

WC Fields

They who drink beer will think beer.

Washington Irving

I drink to make other people more interesting.

George Jean Nathan

Activity

Sloe gin

This activity is a good excuse for a walk and results in an excellent liqueur. Traditionally, sloes for this drink should not be picked until after the first frost, although nowadays you can pick them earlier and put them in the freezer overnight! Pick enough sloes to fill a wine bottle, weigh them and wash them. Half-fill two wine bottles with sloes that you have pricked with a fork. Add half the weight of the sloes in sugar to each bottle and then fill the bottles with gin and cork them. Give the bottle a good shake every few days and then, after 2 months, strain both bottles. This gives you one full bottle of sloe gin. My mother told me the longer you keep it the better it is ... but I have yet to taste an old one! This is a traditional Christmas liqueur, but to be ready for Christmas you need to pick the sloes in October.

Activity

Alcohol quiz

British sailors used to get a daily ration of 'grog'. What is it?

Rum and water

What gives Pernod and ouzo their distinctive flavour?

Aniseed

A Japanese spirit made from rice is called what?

Sake

Why is bourbon called bourbon?

Because it was first made in Bourbon County, Kentucky

Poteen is an illegally distilled Irish drink made from what?

Potatoes

What does VSOP stand for on a bottle of brandy?

Very Special Old Pale

If wine is described as 'brut', how will it taste?

Dry

What is perry made from?

Pears

What is the unique ingredient of mead?

Honey

What is the pub in Coronation Street called?

Rovers Return Inn

What did North American Indians first call whisky?

Firewater

What drink should always be passed to the left?

Port

What is 'uisge beatha', or water of life?

Whisky

What flavour is the liqueur Cointreau?

Orange

From which French region does claret come?

Bordeaux

Which tree's berries are used to flavour gin?

Juniper

What gives advocaat its taste and texture?

Eggs

Which area of France is associated with brandy?

Cognac

What is mixed with champagne to make a 'black velvet'?

Guinness

Which French Benedictine monk from the seventeenth century is popularly credited with inventing champagne?

Dom Pierre Pérignon

Activity

Wine tasting

Ask the local wine society to give your clients a masterclass in wine tasting. What are the different grapes, varieties, regions and tastes? What should we look for in a good bottle of wine, or is it simply a matter of personal taste?

This week's excuse for a party!

Cocktail party

This week is an excuse for an after-dinner cocktail party where everyone gets dressed up in their 'glad rags' and dances to twenties and thirties jazz tunes.

Try making your own cocktails – the recipes given here are taken from an early Foulsham's Universal Cookery Book. Always make a fruit punch for those who do not like alcohol.

Try the alcohol quiz and then sit back and watch a film. The Lost Weekend is a good black-and-white film about an alcoholic, made in 1945 and starring Ray Milland and Jane Wyman. The Roaring Twenties were the cocktail era, and good films depicting this period include the musical Chicago and Some Like it Hot, with Marilyn Monroe, Jack Lemmon and Tony Curtis.

Manhattan

Half-fill a tumbler with broken ice and add ¼ gill of Canadian Club whisky followed by ¼ gill vermouth and a dash of Angostura bitters. Stir well and strain into a cocktail glass. Serve with a cherry.

Sidecar

Half-fill a shaker with broken ice and squeeze into it the juice of quarter of a lemon. Add ¼ gill brandy and ⅛ gill dry gin. Shake well and strain into a cocktail glass.

Week 50   December 10–16

Theme
Hanukkah, health and the dining room

Hanukkah

The Jewish festival of Hanukkah occurs around about now. Hanukkah is also called the Festival of Lights, after a group of Jews in 200 BC wanted to rededicate a temple and only had enough oil for one day but it burned for eight days. An important part of the celebration is the menorah, a candle holder for eight candles. One candle is lit for each night of Hannukah, and after lighting the candle people exchange gifts and eat latkes or potato pancakes. These are cooked in oil in remembrance of the miracle. Sufganiyot, which are doughnuts, are also eaten. Children also play with a dreidel, which is a spinning top inscribed with the Hebrew letters nun, gimmel, hei and shin, an acronym for Nes Gadol Hayah Sham, meaning 'a great miracle happened there'. This is in remembrance of the Jews reclaiming the Holy Land. Parents also make gifts of Hanukkah gelt (money or chocolate coins) to the children.

Latkes

Finely grate four large potatoes and one large onion. Mix three eggs, ½ cup flour and a large pinch of salt in with the vegetables. Fry dollops of the mixture in hot oil and serve them with a sweet apple sauce.

Sufganiyot

Whisk two eggs with 4 tbsp sugar then add 1 tsp vanilla essence and

Speechmark

2 cups low-fat plain yoghurt and blend. Add 3 cups flour and 3 tbsp baking powder and mix into a batter. Drop dollops into hot oil and cook them on both sides for a couple of minutes until they are golden and swollen. Drain them on kitchen paper to get rid of excess oil. Poke a hole in one side with a knife and squeeze in jam. Sprinkle with icing sugar and enjoy.

Activity

Oral hygiene

In a book about food it is expedient to at least give some space and thought to taking care of our teeth. Use a dentist or dental hygienist to give the group a talk and advice as to how best to look after their teeth and dentures. What foods are good, how and when to brush teeth, why and how to 'floss' and what good does fluoride do? These are just a few of the interesting questions that could be asked. It is good to hear a dentist explain what can and can't be done and what the modern dental techniques and equipment are. The dentist could bring along some of that vast array of weapons he or she uses and explain what they are for. Common ailments and problems can be explored and there is also the opportunity for a question-and-answer session.

Activity

Diet and healthy eating quiz

Having examined our teeth, how much do we know about what is good to put in our mouths?

What percentage of your body is water?

70 per cent

What can't coeliacs eat?

Gluten

Are baked beans high or low in fibre?

High

Guinness is good for you! True or false?

Depends how much you drink!

How many portions of fruit and vegetables should you eat a day?

Five

What mineral is good for your teeth and bones?

Calcium

Red meat and green vegetables are a good source of what?

Iron

Which has more fat, red or white meat?

White

Which fats are better for you, saturated or unsaturated?

Unsaturated

What method of cooking is most unhealthy?

Frying

Which contains the most vitamin C, oranges or sprouts?

Sprouts

Which meat is good for your brain?

Fish

What food group is our main source of energy?

Carbohydrates

What food group builds our muscles?

Proteins

What vitamin can be made by the skin in sunlight?

Vitamin D

Scurvy is caused by a lack of which vitamin?

Vitamin C

Rice is a good source of what?

Protein

Too much salt will raise your what?

Blood pressure

Which fruit contains the most fat?

Avocado

How many calories are there in a glass of water?

None

Activity

The dining room

There are a whole range of jobs and tasks centred on the dining room and the ritual of dining, and these can provide the opportunity to give someone a role. One obvious role is that of being in charge of the care of the dining room generally, keeping it neat and tidy and looking nice. The dining room should look like and have the feel of a classy restaurant, because for many people in care, meal times are one of the most enjoyable aspects of the day. If a client takes on the role of keeping the dining room looking good, they should be supported with funds for things like flowers for the tables, serviettes, and so forth. Another key function is the task of laying the tables. This would allow someone to take pride in their work, by ensuring that each place setting is neat and cheerful. It is a useful job and one that will be appreciated by and will likely draw the praise of others. Perhaps next on the list is the less than desirable task of clearing up after a meal. It may be that no one wants to do this, but it just might be that this gives someone the opportunity to contribute usefully and feel wanted and included. You could always lighten this task by doing it as a job-share between a client and a carer – this could also give you the opportunity to get to know the client that much better.

This week's excuse for a party!

School party

Develop a relationship with the local school and invite a class to bake some supper cakes for the clients. They could also prepare a quiz for the group. In return the clients let the children ask them questions about the old days. This would be in keeping with the tradition of oral history, with recollections being handed down from one generation to the next. It might also form part of a school project. The clients could bake for the children too and provide the lemonade. Evenings such as these might well develop into regular events if an enthusiastic teacher is involved.

Speechmark

Week 51 December 17–23

Theme

Fish and chips

Great Britain is an island with a large coastline and so fishing has always been an important source of food in Britain. By the 1920s there were around 35,000 fish and chip shops in the UK, and on 20 December back in 1929, Harry Ramsden opened his first chip shop in a hut in Guiseley, near Bradford. For many years this was the world's largest fish and chip shop! For many people, Fridays became regular 'fish and chip' nights because of religious practices of abstinence from other meat on Fridays. Another essential part of the British 'obsession' with fish and chips is mushy peas. Many will agree that to be enjoyed at their best, the fish and chips have to be sprinkled with salt, doused with vinegar and wrapped in newspaper. They also taste better eaten outdoors on a cold winter's night.

Sir Walter Raleigh brought the potato back to the UK from America, and it was the French who first cut potatoes into strips and fried them, though the Belgians also lay claim to this. Eventually chips as a meal became a staple part of the working man's diet, and in the Second World War fish and chips were important in supplementing the diet, as fish were not rationed. However, trawling was dangerous and there were often fish shortages, so when the 'chippy' did get fish, long queues often formed and of course the price went up! It is a matter of personal taste as to which is the best fish for fish and chips, cod or haddock and over the years the fish shop has expanded its range of products to include fish cakes, battered sausages and even deep-fried battered Mars bars! The meal, despite being fried, is still a good source of protein and vitamins and it remains one of the nation's favourite meals.

Fish cakes

Take a piece of cold boiled haddock or cod and flake it, removing the skin and bones. Mash some cold boiled potatoes and mix this with the fish, adding salt and pepper to taste and a little lemon juice. Mix this into a paste with a beaten egg and 1 oz butter. Form the mixture into cakes and roll them in flour, then in beaten egg and finally in breadcrumbs. Fry in oil for about 4 to 5 minutes each side.

Fish pudding

Skin and bone a cold boiled fish and mash it up with cold boiled potatoes. Add a large dollop of margarine, one beaten egg, salt, pepper, 1 tsp mustard and a little milk and bake it in a tin for 30 minutes in a hot oven.

Fish and wine soup

Poach pieces (around 500 g) of filleted and skinned cod in a bottle of white wine for about 5 minutes until fish starts to break up. Strain the fish. Fry a chopped onion in olive oil and, when soft, add two tins chopped tomatoes with herbs and salt and pepper to taste. Add this to the wine and boil for 10 minutes, and then add the fish and simmer for another 5 minutes. Serve the soup with French bread.

Activity

Feeding the birds

At this time of year, with winter cold weather looming, it is a good idea to begin to think about feeding the birds. This activity can give many people pleasure over a long period of time. Hang a bag of peanuts on a branch near a window so that everyone can watch the birds from their chairs inside. You could also buy a bird table or try making your own – the birds will not be fussy and the building of the bird table will be a useful project for some clients. Do not forget to include a water container too, as water is as important as food. Put up a poster of common garden birds and start to keep a list of birds you have seen. Buy a bird book, invest in a pair of binoculars and soon you will be hooked!

Activity
More eating and food quotations

A man hath no better thing under the sun,
Than to eat, and to drink, and to be merry.

The Bible

A nickel will get you on the subway, but garlic will get you a seat!

American proverb

Hunger is the best sauce in the world.

Miguel de Cervantes Saavedra

You are what you eat.

Anon

The more you eat, the less flavour;
The less you eat; the more flavour.

Chinese proverb

After dinner sit a while; After supper walk a mile.

English saying

He who does not mind his belly, will hardly mind anything else.

Samuel Johnson

This week's excuse for a party!

Fish supper

This week's supper party takes little organisation other than collecting the order and visiting the local 'chippy'. Have plenty of salt and vinegar for clients to use and then eat the fish and chips out of the paper. Films to watch with a fishing theme include *The Perfect Storm* and *Moby Dick*, but the best is the 1990 made-for-TV film *The Old Man and the Sea*. This film of Ernest Hemingway's book stars Anthony Quinn as Santiago, an old fisherman who battles the seas and sharks to bring home a prize marlin.

Week 52 December 24–31

Theme

Christmas food

With December 25 being Christmas Day, our theme this week is an obvious one. Begin by asking the group to think of all the special types of food they associate with Christmas and write these down on a flip chart. You will come up with the likes of mince pies, yule logs, stollen and Christmas puddings and cakes. Allow clients to reminisce about Christmas generally, and tease out any customs and traditions they had in their families. Did they put a sixpence in the Christmas pudding? To convince the children, did they leave a mince pie, brandy and some carrots out for 'Santa' and his reindeer? Ask about family meals and what your clients' favourite Christmas treats and indulgences were. Here are recipes for two Christmas essentials.

Mince pies

Make ½ lb shortcrust pastry and line tart tins with it. Mix ½ lb mincemeat with 2 tbsp brandy and add it to the tarts. Cut out small pastry tops, dip them in milk and place them on top of the tarts. Prick the pastry tops with a fork and press the edges down to seal the pies. Bake the pies for around 15–20 minutes at 425°F.

Christmas pudding

Recipes here vary according to locality and taste. This is an old Lincolnshire farm worker's recipe and was often made a year in advance and hung all year to mature!

Mix together 1 lb each of flour, suet, raisins, currants, sultanas and brown sugar. Mix in 2 oz grated orange peel, 1¼ lb breadcrumbs,

½ lb boiled grated carrots, the grated rind and juice of one lemon, a 'little' nutmeg and a chopped, cored and peeled apple. Mix in three beaten eggs and a little milk to help it bind. Put this into a greased pudding basin, cover it with greased paper and tie it up in a pudding cloth and steam it in a pan of boiling water for 6 hours. Remove the old cloth and paper and recover the pudding with a fresh covering and store in a cool, dry place. When the pudding is required, re-steam it for 2 hours. This recipe will make up to four puddings.

Activity

Christmas food word scrambles

Cinem Sepi	*Mince pies*
Nellost	*Stollen*
Hircstams Kace	*Christmas cake*
Mulp Didpung	*Plum pudding*
Bydran retbut	*Brandy butter*
Luye gol	*Yule log*
Debra cause	*Bread sauce*
Gase nad nooni ffustnig	*Sage and onion stuffing*
Yekurt	*Turkey*
Surbels tuspors	*Brussel sprouts*
Stora snarppsi	*Roast parsnips*
Bracyerrn useca	*Cranberry sauce*

Activity

Carol and Christmas song quiz

Ask what gifts were given in the song 'The Twelve Days of Christmas'. So … on the twelfth day of Christmas my true love sent to me …?

- A partridge in a pear tree

- Two turtle doves

- Three French hens

- Four calling birds

- Five gold rings

- Six geese a-laying

- Seven swans a-swimming

- Eight maids a-milking

- Nine ladies dancing

- Ten lords a-leaping

- Eleven pipers playing

- Twelve drummers drumming

The next quiz centres on lines from carols and Christmas songs to stimulate the memory and it also doubles as an opportunity for a sing-song. Make sure you have a CD of Christmas songs at hand to sing along to. So from which carol or song do the following lines come?

The cattle are lowing
'Away in a Manger'

Then one foggy Christmas Eve, Santa came to say
'Rudolph the Red-Nosed Reindeer'

Good tidings we bring to you and your kin
'We Wish You a Merry Christmas'

In fields where they lay
'The First Noel'

Deep and crisp and even
'Good King Wenceslas'

Not only green when summer's here, but also when 'tis cold and
drear
'O Christmas Tree'

All is calm, all is bright
'Silent Night'

And all the bells on earth shall ring
'I Saw Three Ships (Come Sailing In)'

All seated on the ground
'While Shepherds Watched'

Where the treetops glisten and children listen
'White Christmas'

Sleigh bells ring, are you listening?
'Winter Wonderland'

Let nothing you dismay
'God Rest Ye Merry Gentlemen'

DECEMBER

Peace on earth and mercy mild

   'Hark the Herald Angels Sing'

Earth stood hard as iron, water like a stone

   'In the Bleak Midwinter'

Where a mother laid her baby in a manger for his bed

   'Once in Royal David's City'

O'er the fields we go, laughing all the way

   'Jingle Bells'

Fa la la la la, la la la la

   'Deck the Halls'

Here we come a-wandering so fair to be seen

   'The Wassail Song'

Gloria, Hosanna in excelsis!

   'Ding Dong Merrily on High'

Oh the weather outside is frightful, but the fire is so delightful

   'Let It Snow'

DECEMBER

This week's excuse for a party!

Carol concert

A carol concert is a marvellous opportunity to invite as many relatives and friends as you can. A traditional carol concert helps to combat some of the commercialism that has crept into the season. Serve your mince pies along with sherry or home-made fruit punch and some crackers to pull with hats and jokes to get people in the party mood. It's also a good idea to have your Christmas song quiz to get people in the mood for some singing. Another idea is to arrange for a local school or church choir to come and give you a recital, to make more of an occasion of it. Formalising the event also gives you a good excuse for many fringe group activities such as baking and making drinks.

RESOURCES

Fast Food

Puddings

Fish and Chips

Roast Dinner

Indian Food

Resources

The most important factor for successful group work and activity is beyond doubt the enthusiasm of the staff. Enthusiastic staff can turn an otherwise humdrum activity into an enjoyable and stimulating social event. There is also one other factor that can enhance group work enormously, making it more stimulating and varied, and this is the use of good props.

Many props can be obtained free from travel agents, tourist offices and libraries, and the wise activity organiser will be a frequent visitor to second-hand bookshops. Here can be had a variety of old entertainment and sports annuals and other large, colourful picture books covering a wide range of subjects. Car boot sales and cheap antique shops are also good sources of bygone objects that make good visual and tactile props to stimulate much recall and reminiscence. Of course, the internet is a remarkable place to find practically everything about anything and so time spent browsing online will be time well spent. However, there are certain resources that are prepared with reminiscence and activity specifically in mind and these are well worth seeking out. Speechmark Publishing and Winslow Press are good sources of purpose-made activity and reminiscence materials. They produce a wide range of these and because they are designed with reminiscence and activity with older adults in mind they are very effective. Here is a selection of materials that will complement the activities in this book.

- **Reminiscence grocery cards.** These are large, coloured picture cards in the shape of grocery items.

- **Food colour library.** These are large, coloured picture cards of food items – including categories such as fruit, vegetables, drinks, snacks, basics and prepared foods – and are useful for a wide range of different activities.

- **Snack time.** These are coloured cards showing a range of food and drinks related to food snacks.

Another useful source is the Imperial War Museum's website *The Ministry of Food* (http://food.iwm.org.uk/).